· GARDENING · BY · DESIGN ·

FRAGRANT GARDENS

· JANE · TAYLOR ·

Ward Lock Limited · London

ACKNOWLEDGEMENTS

The publishers gratefully acknowledge the following for granting permission to reproduce the colour photographs: the Harry Smith Horticultural Photographic Collection (front cover and pp 4, 17, 20, 24, 32, 33, 37, 41, 52, 57, 60, 61, 64 and 68); Pat Brindley (pp 9, 21, 29, 40, 44 and 69); Jane Taylor (back cover and pp 8, 12, 48, 49, 56 and 65). John Heseltine took the photograph on p 1 and the remaining photographs were taken by Bob Challinor.

The publishers are especially grateful to the following garden owners for granting permission to photograph their gardens: Mr and Mrs D. Simmons (p 16); Mr and Mrs A. N. Sturn (p 73); and Mr and Mrs A. E. Pedder (p 36).

All the line drawings were drawn by Rosemary Wise.

House editor Denis Ingram
Text set in Bembo
by TJB Photosetting Ltd, South Witham, Lincolnshire

Printed and bound in France by Brodard

British Library Cataloguing in Publication Data

Taylor, Jane
    Fragrant gardens. ——Gardening by design)
    1. Gardens, Fragrant
    I. Title   II. Series
    635'.7   SB454.3.F7
    ISBN 0-7063-6549-6

CONTENTS

Aromatic plants among paving release their fragrance when gently trodden on.

PREFACE

Fragrance can be an element in garden design, just as much as the colour of flower or leaf, the form and outline of your plants, the interplay of light and shadow in your garden. Yet how often one walks into an otherwise delightful garden, only to find that this extra dimension of scent is entirely absent. Even roses seem, all too often, to be chosen for their bright colours rather than their fragrance. Bedding plants are used like ribbons or patches of colour, with – most likely – only sweet alyssum contributing any scent.

Yet proof that we all love fragrance can be found, if proof is needed, in the old bush of mock orange or lilac, long overdue for replacement, but kept for its sweet and heady scent.

Again, our love of fragrance is evident in the pots of scented-leaved geraniums many people cherish on their windowsills, and pinch as they pass.

In more than one garden I know, lily-of-the-valley runs madly into gravel paths, scorning the cosy bed prepared for it, and is tolerated for the poignantly sweet posies it gives us in spring. And though the bed of roses is vivid with scarlets and vermilions and flame-orange, soulless, scentless things, plenty of gardeners still give room as well to an old, crimson velvet climbing rose or a bush of the little, once-flowering Scotch briar with its double, cupped rosettes and unique sweet scent. How well I remember, as a little girl, picking bowls of these little roses and trying in vain to make rose water from them. I recognize, now, how fortunate I was to grow up in a garden where fragrance was welcomed, sought after, and never simply taken for granted.

J.T.

INTRODUCTION: FRAGRANCE IN GARDEN DESIGN

Just as much as colour awareness, an eye for design, or an ear for music, the sense of smell can be developed. Very few people are unlucky enough to have none at all. For most of us, a little training will make an amazing difference.

Perhaps more than anything else that acts upon our five senses, smells produce an emotional as much as a sensory reaction. There can't be many of us who do not know from personal experience how evocative a particular fragrance can be.

One of the difficulties in writing about fragrance is that there is no vocabulary to define scents. They either have to be likened to something else – lemon, almond, vanilla, violet, clove and so on – or else we fall back on the banal 'sweetly scented', 'strongly fragrant'. This difficulty is reflected in the names botanists have given plants – but at least we often have a guide to fragrance in the names they choose.

Epithets like *fragrans*, or the emphatic form *fragrantissimus*, *odorus*, *odoratus*, and *odoratissimus*, and *suavis* meaning 'sweet-scented', all suggest a plant worthy of our consideration. *Moschatus* tells us that the plant is musk-scented, *citriodorus* that it smells of lemon. *Pungens* implies a strong scent, which could be pleasant or unpleasant.

Look out, then, for these botanical hints, and you will find that the extra dimension of fragrance in your garden begins to expand in your awareness. You may well decide consciously to include fragrance as an element in your garden design, as I have already suggested it can and should be.

Immediately a choice imposes itself. Do you make a special garden within a garden, a little corner just for scent, or do you include fragrant plants everywhere in your beds and borders?

To some extent the answer lies in the kind of garden you have and the way you live. If you have a sheltered garden, spared the buffeting winds that can blow fragile perfumes away before you can seize them, you are lucky – you can plant for fragrance everywhere. If on the other hand your garden is exposed you may well do best to contrive a special, sheltered area, protected by hedges or screens of living plants (which can themselves be fragrant).

Commuters will do well to concentrate on evening scents, to be enjoyed at dusk after a long office day.

Some plants are free with their scent and can be set back from a path or lawn to waft their perfume across to you. Others release their fragrance only when you almost bury your nose in them, or physically brush against them. These need to be planted where you can stroke them as you pass, or bend to inhale their fragrance.

Scented plants needn't be limited to conventional beds and borders. You can plant them in containers, to be set perhaps on a patio where you sit out in summer. Among the paving stones of the patio or a path you can put plants that release their perfume when trodden on. Tread gently, just softly scuff them with your toe, to enjoy the fragrance of creeping mint, chamomile, thyme or pennyroyal scuttling along the cracks between the stones.

Add to your garden the extra dimension of fragrance, and soon every plant will be paying rent for its space twice, thrice, four times over in beauty and the poignant appeal of scent.

PART I

SPRING

1

EARLY SPRING

So many trees and shrubs, and such a multitude of bulbs, flower in spring that we can virtually guarantee a mass of colour in our gardens at this season. Faced with such an assault on our senses it is all too easy to overlook fragrance. For all that, there are scents and smells that capture the essence of spring. To me one of the most nostalgic of all smells is not a floral one, but the smell of rain on dry soil in spring. So often, after drying spring winds the garden seems to respond gratefully to the rain when it comes and an indescribably fresh, clean aroma fills the air.

But what can we do to guarantee scent in the spring garden? We must select our trees and shrubs, our bulbs, our little lowly spring flowers, with this in mind.

EARLY CHERRIES AND MAGNOLIAS

Cherries and magnolias are perhaps the typical trees of spring, but I wonder how many people choose them especially for their fragrance?

The earliest of all cherries – unless you count the winter-flowering *Prunus subhirtella autumnalis* – is *Prunus conradinae*. This elegant little tree needs a sheltered position to give us its white or pink-blushed flowers in earliest spring. In such a cosy corner, of course, its sweet fragrance will not be buffeted away by the spring winds. A little later, but still in advance of the main explosion of cherry blossom, comes *Prunus × yedoensis*, a graceful small tree of arching habit, treasured for its masses of almond-scented blush-white flowers. Its variety 'Ivensii', with long, weeping branches decked with a snowfall of pure white flowers, is well worth seeking out.

In some seasons the Japanese apricot, *Prunus mume*, may anticipate *Prunus conradinae*, but normally it flowers a little later. The wild type has single, almond-scented pink flowers that pale as they age. Several varieties can now be had of this pretty small tree, some more fragrant than others. 'Beni-shi-don', for example, has rich warm pink flowers, double and cup-shaped, that are hyacinth-scented. 'Alboplena' is double white, 'O-moi-no-wac' a semi-double white that sports the occasional petal, or even whole flower, in pink. There is also a pale pink flowered weeping form, 'Pendula'.

Decidedly uncommon is *Prunus pseudocerasus* 'Cantabrigiensis', with a very early display of fragrant pink flowers. A hybrid of *P. pseudocerasus* is named 'Wadai' and makes a twiggy tree with deep pink buds opening to pale pink flowers scented, I am told, of ripe peaches. Only by mentioning these unusual trees, and creating a demand for them at local nurseries and garden centres, will we be able to ensure their survival for the decoration and enhancement of our gardens.

Narcissus 'Minnow', a miniature jonquil, grows best in a sunny spot.

The Loderi rhododendrons – here, 'King George' – have huge, white or pale pink, sweetly fragrant flowers

Only a few of the Japanese cherries can be classed as flowering in *early* spring, and some offer more than the characteristic slight scent of this group. Such is 'Hatazakura', with single white or blush flowers, the petals curiously frayed at the edges. 'Washi-no-o' has white flowers sweetly scented and appearing early.

Again, most magnolias will belong in the next chapter. One that is early enough to receive mention here is the yulan, *Magnolia denudata* (syn. *M. conspicua*). Though a little more demanding than the well-known *Magnolia* × *soulangiana* of which it is a parent, it is worth every care. Forming a large shrub, even a small tree in time, it is one of the most beautiful things we can have in the garden when its bare branches are decked with large, pure white, fragrant chalice-shaped flowers.

Magnolia kobus is easy to grow, but demands your patience, for it takes twelve years or so to flower. Then its slightly fragrant white flowers are charming. Its hybrid with *Magnolia stellata*, the well-loved star magnolia, is called *M.* × *loebneri*. Here is a shrubby tree with many narrow-petalled, white, fragrant flowers appearing even on young plants. The selection 'Merrill' has larger, scented white flowers.

Much more fragrant than these is the exquisite *Magnolia salicifolia*, a little tree with slender white flowers powerfully scented of orange blossom. To this quality it adds aromatic leaves, bark and wood, lemon or aniseed scented. Hybrids of this and *M. kobus* are 'Kewensis' and 'Wada's Memory', and both are fragrant. This is the same Wada, incidentally, a Japanese nurseryman, as *Prunus* 'Wadai' is named after; any plant bearing his name is worth seeking for.

The pink-flowered Asiatic magnolias are much sought after. Especially sweetly scented is *M. sprengeri diva*, with rich carmine-pink flowers like huge chalices.

SHRUBS

There are many fragrant shrubs for spring. Early in the season comes the honey scent from the lemon yellow flowers of *Berberis sargentiana*, free on the air – which is as well, for who would wish to bury their nose in so prickly a shrub? Also honey-sweet and free with their scent are the tree heaths, *Erica arborea* and *E. arborea alpina*. *Cornus mas*, looking a little like a witch hazel though unrelated, has a sharp, slightly spicy scent from its little, spiky yellow flowers. The greenish white currant-like flowers of *Osmaronia cerasiformis* are redolent of almonds.

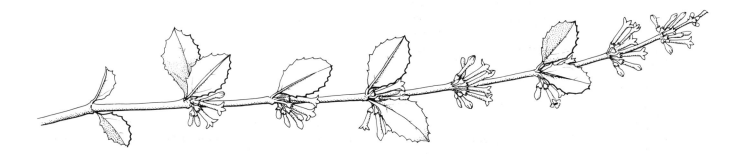

Osmanthus delavayi

All the osmanthuses are deliciously fragrant. *O. delavayi*, with neat polished dark green leaves and clusters of white flowers like tiny jasmine blossoms, is extremely sweet in early spring, and so is its offspring *O. × burkwoodii* (*Osmarea burkwoodii*). The other parent of this, *Osmanthus decorus* (*Phillyrea decora*) is also fragrant.

Perhaps the most powerfully scented of all shrubs for early spring are the male *Skimmia japonica* forms, 'Fragrans' and 'Rubella', with their almost overwhelming fragrance of lily-of-the-valley that wafts on the air.

Not everyone likes the smell of the flowering currant, *Ribes sanguineum*: it has been rudely likened to tomcat! Its relative, the yellow-flowered *R. odoratum*, is clove-scented, and little *R. alpinum* also gives off a sweet scent.

Early spring shrubs that are gaining popularity are the fragrant *Corylopsis*. The daintiest, and earliest, is *C. pauciflora*, a little shrub rather like a miniature hazel in leaf, with primrose yellow, cowslip-scented flowers. With smaller flowers held in larger clusters are its larger-growing relatives, *C. willmottiae* and *C. veitchiana*. The first has showy soft yellow flowers; its form 'Spring Purple' adds the bonus of plum-purple young foliage. *C. veitchiana* has lemon yellow flowers enlivened by brick red anthers. Another kind, *C. spicata*, has brighter yellow flowers. All have the scent of cowslips.

You might not think first of willows for fragrance, yet *Salix triandra* is worth growing as much for its almond scent as for its showy clusters of mimosa-like catkins. This large shrub also offers attractive shiny foliage and flaking bark to make a far more worthwhile plant than the overused weeping willow.

BULBS

The bulbs of early spring are many and, in the main, easy to grow. Anyone can have sheets of crocuses, grape hyacinths, daffodils, tulips and dwarf irises. For scent the fragrant kinds of narcissus are hard to beat, the short cupped varieties especially, the little jonquils and tazettas most of all. The tazetta hybrids 'Geranium', 'Cheerfulness' and its yellow companion, and the others, are all deliciously fragrant. All the jonquils are worth seeking out for their sweet scent, and planting in a warm corner.

Iris reticulata in shades of blue, violet and purple; ethereal grey-mauve *Crocus tomasinianus* and the varieties of *C. chrysanthus* in white, yellow, bronze and blue: these all flower early enough almost to qualify as winter flowers. For all that, I feel that by their nature they belong with early spring. All are scented. Some of the *Crocus chrysanthus* forms, indeed, bear a strong resemblance in their scent to the perfume once alleged to be the world's most expensive, 'Joy'. Grow them in great swathes – they are cheap enough for this – to gain the full benefit of their scent. They can be tucked in at the front of borders, in sunny spots among shrubs, or in raised beds, or grown in bowls and brought into the house when in flower.

Later the grape hyacinths appear. The common blue *Muscari* 'Heavenly Blue' is one of the sweetest of the familiar kinds, and cheap enough to grow in masses. Less well known are *M. moschatum* and *M. ambrosiacum*. What a lovely name, the ambrosial one! They are soberly coloured, and deliciously scented; rather expensive, and not for massing. True hyacinths, of course, are loved, and grown indoors, for their perfume. After you have enjoyed them in the house, plant them outside where they will flower again year after year. Soon the flowers will become smaller and more elegant than when first purchased; they will still waft their rich perfume as generously.

VIOLETS AND PRIMROSES

The scent of violets must be known to everyone. Patches of purple and white *Viola odorata* can be drifted among shrubs to fill the air with their fragrance in early spring. If you pick and sniff a violet, the first strong scent when inhaled quickly disappears, for the perfume of violets has the strange property of anaesthetizing the sense of smell for a while.

Smilacina racemosa is a fragrant spring-flowering plant related to Solomon's seal and happy in similar conditions among shrubs

In years gone by Parma violets were grown in many gardens, in sheltering frames, for their richly scented double flowers. Now these old varieties are almost impossible to find, but they are still cherished in a few gardens and perhaps they might regain their popularity in the future if enough of us ask for them.

Primroses, which will grow happily in the same positions as *Viola odorata*, half shaded by shrubs, have a delicate fresh fragrance. For sunnier positions, in well-fed soils, polyanthus and auriculas – both related to primroses – bring a rich tapestry of colour to many gardens in spring, and welcome fragrance as well.

2

LATE SPRING

CHERRIES AND CRABS

The flowers of late spring are more dependable than those of early spring, at least in climates where the spring season is fickle, balmy one day and sharp with frost the next. In such 'stop-go' weather the early cherries may disappoint; the later ones seldom.

Most of the Japanese cherries flower in late spring. All have a trace of scent; some much more. Of these, for this season we could choose from:

'AMANOGAWA' Valuable in very limited space for its narrow outline, this is prized also for its fragrant, shell pink flowers.

'JO-NIOI' A cherry of spreading outline, in complete contrast to 'Amanogawa'. The single white flowers are delectably scented of almonds.

'SHIROTAE' This lovely tree has a wide-spreading habit with branches held horizontally. The large, pure white flowers are sweetly scented.

'TAKI-NIOI' Said to be honey scented, with small but copious white flowers among red-bronze young leaves.

Of cherries other than the Japanese varieties, the St Lucie cherry, *Prunus mahaleb*, is a very pretty tree decked with abundant white fragrant flowers in late spring. Another white-flowered, fragrant cherry is *P. speciosa*, ancestor of many of the Japanese cherries such as 'Shirotae'.

Many flowering crabs are lavish with their scent, and their blossom is beautiful. The enchanting *Malus floribunda* is often planted for its chintzy pink and white flowers opening from cherry red buds, borne in frothing masses on a little arching tree. It also delights with its fresh fragrance. So, too, does the white-flowered Siberian crab, *Malus baccata*, which bears little red or yellow fruits hardly bigger than a berry.

Another fragrant pink and white crab is *Malus spectabilis*, a small tree with upright branches. The variety 'Albiplena' has large white flowers with extra petals, scented like violets.

These come fairly early in the season. Early, too, is 'Profusion', the one to choose if you like the purple-leaved, claret-red-flowered crabs. The scent is light and pleasant. 'Hopa' is another with large wine-red scented flowers; it combines the bloom of the Siberian crab and the impossibly-named *Malus niedzwetzskyana* which put the red colouring into the foliage of so many hybrid crabs.

The season of the flowering crabs extends almost to early summer, with one of the best of all: *Malus coronaria* and its variety 'Charlottae'. These lovely trees have shell-pink flowers, semi-double in the named variety, exquisitely scented of violets. They also give the bonus of rich autumn colour. Allied to *M. coronaria*, and also fragrant, *M. ioensis* and its double form 'Plena' are temperamental, especially on chalky soils. Another violet-scented crab in this group is *M. angustifolia* which has unusual salmon pink colouring unlike the usual candy or carmine pink.

A crab that looks a little like a cherry is the fragrant *Malus hupehensis* which comes in pink or white and bears cherry-like fruits in autumn. For brighter colour, crimson in bud opening to rich pink, and with fragrance too, you could select 'Hillieri'. The semi-double flowers are freely borne on arching branches.

Many of the crabs grown for their fruits, and most apples as well, have at least a faint, elusive scent that is full of nostalgia for people who grew up in orchard areas. With the creation of so many dwarfed forms of apple to fit into modern tiny gardens, this fresh scent has been brought closer to our noses.

OTHER TREES

Cherries and crabs so dominate the floral scene at tree height that some other good things risk being left out. No one, though, is likely to overlook laburnum. Few trees are lovelier when decked with their tresses of softly scented yellow flowers. The variety 'Vossii', very free with its flowers and sparing of its poisonous seeds, is perhaps the most generous with its freesia-like perfume.

The flowering thorns, species of *Crataegus*, smell offensively fishy to some, though the sweetish undertone appeals to others. This controversial smell is shared by many cotoneasters and rowans.

The flowering ashes, *Fraxinus mariesii* and the manna ash, *F. ornus*, flower on the cusp of spring and early summer, their tiny cream flowers in sweetly scented clusters. They make trees of more manageable size than the horse chestnuts. Of these, the common *Aesculus hippocastanum* and its double form 'Baumannii' have more scent than the red-flowered *A. × carnea*.

LILACS

All the large-flowered garden lilacs, and most other lilac species, are delectably fragrant. Among the large-flowered kinds the choice is great, and because all are perfumed the choice can be made on the grounds of colour. Here I want to mention some other lilacs that may be less well known.

First, two small-growing, small-leaved lilacs that, despite their size, distill the essence of lilac from their little trusses of flower. *Syringa velutina* 'Palibin' has mauve flowers; *S. microphylla* is nearer to true pink. Its variety 'Superba' often flowers again in autumn.

A little larger in stature is the Persian lilac, *S × persica*, a graceful and slender shrub that comes with lilac or white flowers. Its hybrid with the parent of the large-flowered garden lilacs is *S × chinensis*, the Rouen lilac. A dense arching shrub, it is decked with big hanging tresses of soft lilac flowers, deliciously scented.

Of the many wild lilac species, most agreeably scented (a few less so, like privet) I want to mention *Syringa sweginzowii*. Despite its cumbersome name this is an enchanting thing with open sprays of pure pale pink flowers and an exquisite perfume.

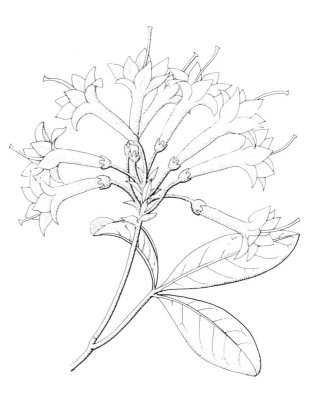

Azalea
'Narcissiflorum'

Sweet rocket (*Hesperis matronalis*) is most fragrant at night when its pale flowers glow in the dim light

Magnolia wilsonii is typical of the summer-flowering magnolias, with nodding, scented flowers

RHODODENDRONS

Another great tribe of spring-flowering shrubs are the rhododendrons. Not all are scented, but a choice few are very fragrant indeed.

Some of the best are a little tender, and included later among greenhouse plants though they will thrive outside in mild gardens. Tough enough for most areas is *Rhododendron decorum*, white or palest shell pink and very sweetly scented. Later comes the similar *R. discolor*.

The blood of two beautiful scented rhododendrons, *R. griffithianum* and *R. fortunei*, is joined in the magnificent Loderi hybrids. These bear big trusses of large, lily-like flowers in white, cream or soft pink. All are wonderfully fragrant.

Azaleas belong botanically in the genus *Rhododendron*. Many of the deciduous kinds are extremely fragrant. The honeysuckle azalea is the name sometimes given to the common yellow azalea *R. luteum*, because of its powerful scent. Of the hybrids, the Ghent and Occidentale kinds are very fragrant, especially in the evening. 'Daviesii' is an old but still charming white, yellow-flared kind. Pink, orange-flushed 'Exquisitum' and the double, primrose yellow 'Narcissiflorum' are also very sweet, as is the Occidentale hybrid 'Superbum', pink with apricot markings.

OTHER SHRUBS FOR SPRING

Some of the finest fragrant shrubs for spring, rivalling in their perfume the lilacs themselves, are the viburnums. Those that flower in spring are carnation- or daphne-scented: *V. carlesii* and *V. × juddii*, *V. × carlcephalum* and the nearly evergreen *V. × burkwoodii* which opens from late winter through the spring. Newer, named kinds are 'Anne Russell', 'Fulbrook' and 'Park Farm Hybrid'. All, parents and offspring alike, have rounded heads of close-packed white or blush flowers opening from pink buds. In 'Aurora' and 'Charis' the pink remains unfaded.

Berberis buxifolia fills the air with its honey perfume, and *Corokia cotoneaster* scents the breeze with chocolate. *Cytisus × praecox* has a strange fragrance, verging on the unpleasant at close quarters. The hardy orange, *Poncirus trifoliata*, has white, orange-blossom-scented flowers, and in the same family *Choisya ternata*, the Mexican orange, has sweetly perfumed white flowers among glossy, pungent foliage.

Lonicera syringantha is a shrubby honeysuckle with little lilac-pink flowers, each like a lilac floret and smelling as sweet. Unbeatable for fragrance are the lowlier daphnes, the spreading pink-flowered *D. cneorum* and its taller, easier offspring *D. × burkwoodii* with paler flowers. Of more compact stature are *D. tangutica*, *D. collina* and *D. sericea*, all with white, purple-tinged flowers in late spring.

CLIMBERS

Allotting flowers to a specific season is always an arbitrary business even if one vaguely says 'late spring' rather than specifying a month. Wisteria, some of which could qualify for inclusion here, is covered in Chapter 3; after all, some wisterias don't flower until after midsummer. But a few climbers genuinely belong to spring, and among them clematis such as *C. alpina* – which has no scent – and *C. armandii* – which has. This vigorous evergreen from China has massed small flowers in white or blush and vanilla-scented.

Hard on its heels comes the much more familiar *Clematis montana*, of which some forms are scented: 'Elizabeth' in pale pink, or the less familiar 'Alexander' in creamy-white.

For beauty these clematis totally eclipse my next climber, but for perfume they cannot compare. *Holboellia latifolia* has handsome, copious evergreen foliage on twining stems, and insignificant little purply brown or greeny buff flowers, but their scent is sheer delight.

Very similar is *Stauntonia hexaphylla*, with fragrant mauve-white flowers in spring. Both these unusual climbers need a sunny, reasonably sheltered wall and make luxuriant growth ideal for concealing a less than lovely structure.

SPRING FLOWERS

Wallflowers have an unmistakable warm scent somewhat like that of pinks or stocks. The little double yellow 'Harpur Crewe', raised by cuttings not seed, is an old cottage garden plant of great charm. Closely related are the species of *Erysimum*. The dwarf yellow *E. alpinum*, and paler 'Moonlight', are cinnamon-scented. Try, too, the slightly tender, palest primrose-coloured, exquisitely perfumed *E. capitatum* for something a little different.

The sweet rocket, *Hesperis matronalis*, has something of the same clove scent, mixed with violet. It comes in pure white or soft lilac, a lovely plant for wildish corners of the garden where it can be left to self-sow. Double forms exist, just, in white and the even rarer lilac; they are, like the double wallflowers, favourite old cottage garden plants now hard to cultivate. They must be propagated by cuttings or by division, and nurtured lovingly for their charm and their delicious perfume.

Little bunches of lily-of-the-valley are the sweetest posies we can pick for the house in late spring. The larger-flowered 'Fortin's Giant' flowers a little later than the ordinary kind, so it is worth growing both, to have the longest possible season of the plant the French call *muguet*.

BULBS

The latest narcissi to flower are the poeticus kinds, white-flowered with tiny cups, often red-rimmed. They are also among the very sweetest. By comparison the scent of tulips is faint, but strongest in some of the orange and yellow Darwin tulips. Bulb merchants should be persuaded to mention the scent of tulips where appropriate; it is a lovely addition to their beauty. Among species tulips, often sold as 'botanical tulips' by those same bulb merchants, are a few that are sweetly scented: the Lady Tulip, slender little carmine and white *T. clusiana*, is one. Another is *T. sylvestris*, a graceful yellow tulip suitable for growing in grass.

The scent of bluebells is delicious, but they are invasive in a small garden, and the better-behaved garden kinds of Spanish bluebell are scarcely scented.

Philadelphus coronarius 'Aureus' is grown as much for its bright lime-yellow foliage as for its delicious mock-orange perfume

The tree lupin, *Lupinus arboreus*, has a rich warm scent and is well suited to seaside gardens

PART II
MIDSUMMER

3
TREES, SHRUBS AND BORDER PLANTS

TREES

By midsummer there are fewer trees in flower, after the cherries and crabs have ended. At this season, though, comes the sweet, carrying perfume of the limes. The common lime is *Tilia × europaea*, a tree too large for most gardens. So, too, are its parents, the large-leaved lime, *T. platyphyllos*, and the small-leaved lime, *T. cordata*, which flowers a little later. Slightly smaller in size than these is the elegant, and aphis-free, *T. × euchlora*. Though in time it, too, gets large, one of the loveliest weeping trees where space permits is the weeping silver lime, *T. petiolaris*, with silvery backed leaves and intensely sweet flowers in later summer.

Other fragrant flowering trees for this season are the false acacias, *Robinia pseudacacia*; and the snowdrop tree, *Styrax japonica*, though neither can rival the limes for scent. The yellowwood, *Cladrastis lutea*, has white flowers rather like the robinia's and more fragrant.

LATE MAGNOLIAS

It is from the summer-flowering magnolias that we can expect the greatest bonus of scent at this season. Easiest to cultivate are four species and one (probable) hybrid that all make large shrubs or small trees, and all have nodding white flowers with crimson stamens.

The choice can depend on soil conditions in your garden. If you are on chalk, choose *Magnolia × highdownensis*. For acid soils, *M. sieboldii* is a good choice and almost as striking in crimson fruit as in flower. On ordinary garden soils, improved as always for magnolias with plenty of humus, *M. wilsonii* or the deliciously lemon-scented *M. sinensis* are first-rate. The last of this group is the uncommon, creamy-white flowered *M. globosa*, with more rounded flowers.

Both *M. hypoleuca* and *M. × watsonii* have creamy flowers, turning almost to buff with age. Both are exquisitely scented. A good tree of the rare *M. × watsonii* would be one of the most precious legacies you could make to future gardening generations, who could enjoy its heady, far-carrying fragrance.

I mention the umbrella tree, *Magnolia tripetala*, by way of warning. When well grown it is most handsome in leaf, but the flowers smell almost offensive to some people and it is, in my experience, hard to keep in good shape, though very cold-resistant.

SHRUBS

Apart from roses, which merit a chapter to themselves, the fragrant garden in summer is dominated by the mock oranges, *Philadelphus* (often, wrongly, called *Syringa*, a name which belongs to lilac). The old mock orange, *P. coronarius*, is a big untidy shrub with powerfully fragrant creamy flowers. Better for garden value are its coloured-leaved forms, the palely gold *P. coronarius* 'Aureus' and white-variegated 'Bowles' Variety'. Put this last one where you can see it at dusk; it glows like moonlight. Although it was called 'Bowles' Variety' after that wonderful old amateur gardener who did so much for the Royal Horticultural Society during his lifetime, Bowles himself had a very sensitive nose and found the perfume of the old mock orange too strong, so much so that he would have the flowers cut off his plants!

Less familiar, but equally sweet, are the felty-leaved *P. delavayi* and neat, small-growing, small-leaved *P. microphyllus*. A favourite of mine, but hard to obtain, is *P. argyrocalyx* which holds its sweetly perfumed white flowers in silvery calyces.

Some of the named hybrid mock oranges are more perfumed than others. Especially good are 'Belle Etoile' with squarish, white, purple-centred flowers, and the very pineapple-scented 'Beauclerk' with big square white flowers. 'Virginal' is a familiar double-flowered kind which grows large; for smaller spaces you could choose the double, creamy white 'Manteau d'Hermine'. Small single-flowered kinds include 'Sybille' with arching branches bearing orange-scented flowers. 'Avalanche' and 'Erectus' are also fairly compact, with small leaves and small but richly perfumed flowers.

Most deutzias, though closely related to the mock oranges, are unscented. You can find exceptions in 'Avalanche', in the pink-flowered 'Rosalind', or hawthorn-scented *D. compacta* and its pretty lilac-flowered variant 'Lavender Time'. But bear in mind that not everyone likes the smell of hawthorn flowers – some of us find them distinctly fishy.

The buddleia season opens with *B. globosa*, bearing its orange ball-shaped clusters of honey-scented flowers on a big, leafy shrub. It cannot compete for fragrance, however, with two members of the pea family that flower at the same time.

Genista cinerea is a beautiful, elegant, yellow-flowered broom of arching habit, weighed down with its masses of small but sweetly scented flowers. More delicious still is the fragrance of the tree lupin, *Lupinus arboreus*, its spikes of pale or lemon yellow, or more rarely white or lavender, perfumed like a beanfield. Easy from seed and fast-growing, this is a most valuable shrub for new gardens, to use in mixed flower borders, or to shelter newly planted, somewhat tender shrubs from wind and frost. With all this, it has beauty and fragrance too. One can hardly ask for more.

And as we are with the pea family, I shall include here a third shrub that flowers on the cusp of mid-and high summer. *Cytisus battandieri* is a broom from North Africa, but very unlike our ordinary conception of a broom. In place of thin, whippy, sparsely leaved stems, it has laburnum-like leaves, except that they are silvery and silky. And instead of the more familiar broom habit of bearing flowers dispersed all along the stems, this one has them concentrated into fat conical clusters, bright yellow in colour and scented of pineapple. At least, this is how it smells to me; but Mr Bowles (of the variegated mock orange, and many other good plants too) discerned in its changing fragrance strawberries, 'grapefruit and lemons' or 'a fruit salad with a dash of maraschino or kirsch. You can get all these scents from the same bunch of blooms at different times of the day'. *Cytisus battandieri* lends itself to wall-training and is often thus seen, but will also form a handsome, bulky, free-standing shrub.

CLIMBING PLANTS

Few climbing plants flower early in the year, though wisteria must be the first to be mentioned here as many are already well in flower by midsummer.

For walls or pergolas, or for clinging into old trees, few climbers are lovelier than wisteria, with its long tresses of pea flowers in lilac-mauve, white or, less commonly, pink. *Wisteria sinensis* is the one most commonly seen; its fragrant flowers are usually blue-mauve but can also be had in white, or dark purple, and in double forms. For extra-long trails you should choose *W. floribunda* 'Macrobotrys' (syn. *W. multijuga*) from Japan; glorious if your garden boasts an arched bridge over a stream, Japanese-style, but equally beautiful on a house wall or decorating a pergola.

Cytisus battandieri is the pineapple broom, with silvery leaves and stubby, fruit–scented yellow flower spikes in summer

Honeysuckle flowering freely on a pole among roses, set off by a formally clipped yew hedge

Sweeter even than wisteria are the jasmines and honeysuckles. *Jasminum officinale* is the perfumed summer jasmine; it has a larger-flowered form, 'Affine', and two variegated-leaved kinds of which 'Aureovariegata' is the showiest. The vigorous, pink-flowered *J.* × *stephanense* is also fragrant.

The honeysuckles with the brightest flowers are scentless, alas, but the others, with flowers of creamy pink, pale gold or red-purple on cream, are deliciously fragrant, especially in the evening. First comes *Lonicera caprifolium*, with cream flowers. Our wild honeysuckle is *L. periclymenum*, and it has a well-known garden form 'Serotina' which flowers over a long season. Less often seen, but just as fragrant, are *L. etrusca* and its hybrid with *L. caprifolium*, *L.* × *americana*. This hybrid, crossed again with the evergreen, but scentless, *L. sempervirens*, has produced the brightest of the scented kinds, *L.* × *heckrotii* 'Gold Flame' with golden yellow flowers flushed orange outside.

These are all deciduous. Evergreen, or semi-evergreen, is the extremely vigorous *L. japonica* and its form 'Halliana' with fragrant white flowers deepening with age to yellow. This is widely available. Not so the magnificent *L. splendida*, with glaucous evergreen foliage and fragrant, creamy yellow flowers with red-purple tips.

LATE-FLOWERING RHODODENDRONS

A choice few rhododendrons flower late, at midsummer or even after, and are scented. *Rhododendron discolor* is a big shrub with large trusses of fragrant pink flowers. As handsome in leaf as in flower is *R. auriculatum*, with great trusses of perfumed white flowers. And if you have a warm garden, with suitable soil, you could plant the hardiest of the Maddenia section, *R. crassum*, with funnel-shaped white or blush flowers.

A cross between *R. auriculatum* and *R. discolor* produced 'Argosy', with very fragrant white flowers. Also with the blood of one or other of these, or allied species, are 'Isabella' and 'July Fragrance', 'Midsummer Snow' and the huge 'Polar Bear', all white-flowered and sweetly fragrant.

HERBACEOUS PERENNIALS FOR FRAGRANCE

Some beautiful early-flowering perennials are valued as much for their perfume as for awakening the summer borders. The great tribe of irises flower ahead of most summer perennials and many bearded irises are fragrant. This is especially true of the old, blue-purple *Iris germanica*, its origins lost in antiquity, and grey-white *I. florentina*, from whose aromatic roots orris root powder is ground – an ingredient in pot pourri. The noble *Iris pallida dalmatica*, with clear lavender blue flowers and broad, glaucous, long-lasting blades of leaf, is also fragrant.

Much less showy than these, but with even more scent, is the plum-tart iris, *I. graminea*, so called because its insignificant little flowers, half-buried among the leaves, smell just like hot stewed plums.

Day lilies, too, may be fragrant. Best of all for scent is *Hemerocallis flava*, the early yellow day lily, and the night-opening *H. citrina*. Mahogany-backed *H. dum—ortieri*, *H. middendorfiana* and *H. multiflora* are also lily-scented, and this is inherited by the superb 'Golden Chimes' with rich gold, maroon-backed flowers. The named yellow-flowered kinds, 'Marion Vaughn', 'Hyperion' and many others, are also sweet-scented.

There is a fragrant columbine, *Aquilegia fragrans*, with creamy-white clove-scented flowers, and a scented delphinium, *D. wellbyi*, a tender charmer with pale verdigris flowers.

For moist soils, choose the giant Himalayan cowslip, *Primula florindae*, which is a willing grower with pale yellow, white-dusted fragrant flowers. Its smaller relatives *P. sikkimensis* in yellow, *P. alpicola* in white, primrose or lilac, deep maroon *P. secundiflora* and the odd, anise-rooted *P. anisodora*, are also sweetly scented.

Iris florentino

PINKS AND CARNATIONS

Most pinks, and the precious old border carnations, have that characteristic warm, clove scent for which they have been prized over the centuries. Despite its misshapen flowers the white *Dianthus* 'Mrs Sinkins' is still popular, and that same scent can accompany pink, crimson, plum-purple and laced flowers. Many of the little so-called alpine pinks are also clove-perfumed. To their lovely flowers they add beautiful glaucous foliage, making them among the most valuable of perennials for decorating the front of the sunny border.

LILIES

Lilies have gained the reputation, not entirely justified, of being difficult aristocrats. Certainly, some are tricky. Others are almost as willing as dandelions to grow. Since its discovery early in the century, *Lilium regale* has become justly popular for the ease with which it can be raised from seed, its huge heads of flared, white flowers enhanced by maroon outer stripes to the petals and the rich golden pollen at their heart, and most of all for its amazing, far-reaching perfume.

The Madonna lily, *L. candidum*, is just as liberal with its sweet perfume, from spires of pure white flowers. Its pale apricot-flowered hybrid, *L. × testaceum*, is rare, expensive, beautiful, and worth every care. Much less aristocratic is the yellow or coppery orange *L. pyrenaicum*, a leafy plant with a heavy fragrance verging on the uncomfortable.

Many other lilies, some belonging to late summer, are fragrant. The catalogue of a good lily grower will list the fragrant kinds.

4

ROSES

THE OLD ROSES

Midsummer is the season of the old roses, which are unequalled in the generosity of their scent. In the garden combine them with pinks and irises, peonies and lilies, and lowly aromatic plants, to create the year's peak of fragrance.

Each kind of old rose has its distinctive perfume, not to be described in words. We have to learn to know for ourselves the fragrance of the gallicas, the damasks, and the moss roses.

The double gallicas are the sweetest. They come in rich colours of crimson velvet as in 'Tuscany', or 'Charles de Mills', which is full of petals and looks like the underside of a mushroom. Paler shades of mauve and violet and lavender are also gallica colours. Of this tender colouring are 'Belle de Crécy' and the white-striped 'Camaieux'.

Damask roses all incline to paler colours, white or blush. 'Mme Hardy' is an exquisite full-petalled, flat-faced white with a green eye. 'Leda' is white also, the petal edges smudged with red.

The alba or white roses are not all white. Most powerfully scented of all is 'Great Maiden's Blush', a large shrub. 'Céleste' is exquisite, shell pink, opening from scrolled buds. Of richer tones, carmine fading to shell pink, is 'Queen of Denmark' (more often listed as 'Königin von Dänemark'). With the Provence or centifolia roses, sometimes called cabbage roses, we are back to pinks and carmines and an unparalleled richness of perfume. 'Fantin Latour', named after the great French painter, has flowers of exquisite pale pink. Deeper in colour, near to magenta, is 'Tour de

Malakoff'. The crested moss, 'Cristata', has pink flowers set in crested calyces.

'Cristata' is not a true moss. This name is kept for roses distinguished by the sticky, fragrant, 'mossy' appearance of the calyx and flower stalk. The common moss has pink flowers; 'Blanche Moreau' is white. Much taller than these is the old velvet moss, 'William Lobb', unique in his grey-lilac colouring. Almost black-crimson, with dark moss, is 'Nuits de Young', which needs pale yellow flowers to set it off – a pale bearded iris perhaps.

Derived from a British native rose, many forms of the Scotch or burnet roses, *R. spinosissima*, have double, cupped flowers that give them an old-fashioned look. 'Double White' and 'Double Blush' are survivors of many hundreds that were once popular.

With the Bourbon, Portland and hybrid perpetual roses we come to shrubs that look old-fashioned but have a second season of flower. The Portlands, indeed – intensely fragrant 'Comte de Chambord' and others – are almost perpetual. Among Bourbons we could choose lilac-pink 'Louise Odier' or mauve 'Reine des Violettes'. 'La Reine Victoria' and her paler, blush-white companion 'Mme Pierre Oger' have exquisite cupped flowers.

To the Bourbons, too, belong the thornless roses 'Zéphyrine Drouhin' and paler pink 'Kathleen Harrop'. But perhaps the most powerfully scented of all roses is 'Mme Isaac Pereire', a Bourbon with huge carmine flowers.

Hybrid perpetuals are less grown now; the older generation may remember red 'General Jack' ('Général Jacqueminot') or the delicious pink 'Mrs John Laing'. A cottage garden hybrid perpetual with candy pink

For the longest tresses of flower, choose *Wisteria floribunda* 'Macrobotrys'

flowers, still sometimes seen, is 'John Hopper'.

The family of *Rosa chinensis* gave the Bourbon and later roses their repeat-flowering character. 'Old Blush China' bears pink flowers, scented of sweet peas, over a long season.

Another line in breeding resulted in the hybrid musks, superb garden shrubs that fit in virtually any setting. One of the original hybrid musks was 'Trier', with small white, yellow-eyed flowers exquisitely scented. Larger-flowered kinds are 'Buff Beauty', the colour of ripe apricots and and honey; clear pink 'Cornelia', creamy white 'Moonlight' and blush 'Penelope', all richly musk-scented. Their perfume carries freely on the air.

MODERN SHRUB ROSES

Modern shrub roses are a variable lot. All I can do is mention a few, chosen for their fragrance.

'Cerise Bouquet', with small cerise-red flowers, is scented of raspberries, pink 'Constance Spry' of myrrh. So too is 'Magenta', ineptly named for it is grey-lilac in colour. Raspberry is mixed with banana in the scent of deep pink 'Kathleen Ferrier'. Spicier perfumes belong to the clove-scented, coral-pink 'Fritz Nobis' and the 'Frühlings' group – 'Frühlingsgold' is the best known and combines oranges and oriental spices in its fragrance. 'Golden Wings' is another scented rose with single, wide yellow flowers. 'Maigold', with double flowers of yolk yellow and buff, is also richly scented.

The salmon pink and apricot 'Nymphenburg' has a powerful fragrance of fresh apples. And lastly I must mention 'Macrantha' and its rare hybrid 'Macrantha Daisy Hill', with single flowers, pale pink fading to cream and delectably fragrant. Both have bright red hips for autumn display.

WILD SPECIES ROSES

Many species roses give us two displays in the same way as 'Macrantha', flowers then hips. Again, I can

select only a few.

For fragrance and ease of cultivation, the rugosa roses are hardly to be beaten. Among fresh green, crinkled foliage they bear single or double flowers of pure paper white – as in 'Blanc Double de Coubert' – pink ('Frau Dagmar Hastrup', a single) or rich magenta, such as the double 'Roseraie de l'Hay'. All are recurrent-flowering; the singles give us tomato-red hips in autumn as well.

Two rose species have fragrant foliage, the aroma carrying on the air. The sweet briar, *Rosa rubiginosa*, gives freely of its scent of stewed apples, and has fragrant flowers as well. *Rosa primula* is called the incense rose because of its aromatic foliage.

CLIMBING ROSES

A great group of wild climbing roses, and their garden derivatives, the synstylae roses, have much fragrance to delight us. Choose from the orange-scented 'Wedding Day' or 'Polyantha Grandiflora', the banana fragrance of *Rosa longicuspis*, or fruity *R. multiflora*. 'Bobbie James' and 'Rambling Rector' are very vigorous.

All these share, apart from their vigour, large clusters of many small milk-white, yellow-centred flowers. Larger in flower is the rambler 'Francis E. Lester', scented of oranges and bananas like the buff-yellow, small-flowered 'Goldfinch'. 'Paul's Himalayan Musk' is also small-flowered, in lilac pink, with a good *multiflora* scent.

Of the half-dozen or so 'blue' ramblers, violet-mauve 'Veilchenblau' is the only one to be fragrant, and has a scent reminiscent of green apples.

The shining-leaved *luciae* ramblers are typified by 'Albéric Barbier' in creamy white from near-yellow buds, with a green apple scent. The same fragrance belongs to coral-pink 'François Juranville'. 'Gerbe Rose' in lilac pink is peony-scented. And everyone knows 'Albertine', with her coppery pink flowers and rich tea fragrance.

The old noisette and tea roses are not much grown now. 'Gloire de Dijon', buff yellow warmed with apricot, lives on in D.H. Lawrence's poem, 'Glory Roses', and for its rich perfume. 'Climbing Lady Hillingdon' is apricot yellow in colour, and apricot-scented too. Miniature-flowered 'Climbing Cécile Brunner' is a poppet with perfect thimble-sized pale pink hybrid tea blooms and a sweet scent.

Rosa 'Cecile Brunner'

Among full-sized hybrid-tea-flowered climbers, 'New Dawn' has shell pink scented flowers of exquisite form. Best loved perhaps for their fragrance are the red roses, 'Climbing Etoile de Hollande' and 'Guinée', with the rich velvety perfume you expect in a deep red rose.

BEDDING AND BUSH ROSES

For the hybrid teas themselves, and for floribundas (or large-flowered and cluster-flowered roses, as they are now termed) it is perhaps best to consult a rose grower's catalogue. Among many names to look out for are older kinds retained for their lovely perfume: 'Fragrant Cloud', 'Ena Harkness', 'Mme Louis Laperrière', 'Papa Meilland', 'Wendy Cussons' – and older than all these, exquisite scrolled soft pink 'Ophelia', dating from 1912.

A new cluster-flowered rose that was launched with justifiable pride in its fragrance is milk-white 'Margaret Merril'.

FRAGRANT ROSES IN THE GARDEN

As is evident from even this brief account of fragrant roses, they vary greatly in character, and in the ways we can use them in our gardens. The old roses assort best with other old-fashioned, even cottage flowers such as the double mock orange, Chinese peonies, irises, and old-fashioned pinks – all contributing their quota of perfume to a planting scheme suitable for cottage or grand garden alike.

The wild species climbing roses, and those named kinds that share their untamed grace, are best displayed in a natural way, flung through a tree perhaps – an old apple tree could find a new lease of life in this role, or something larger for the most vigorous roses. For a

Yellow day-lilies are the sweetest. 'Golden Chimes' has small but abundant flowers, the petals backed with mahogany

Primula florindae is the giant Himalayan cowslip, with sweetly scented flowers

pergola or an arch, garden ramblers and climbers are best, and if you love these roses you may well make room, somehow, for such a structure, and build your garden design around it. For an arch a rose such as 'Adélaide d'Orléans', which has hanging clusters of pink flowers, would be more suitable than one which holds its flowers stiffly upright. Pillar roses could adorn the uprights of a pergola, and the more supple, graceful ramblers the cross-bars; or you could use ropes to link the uprights, the roses' flexible stems trained along the ropes each year.

For warm, sunny house walls there are many exquisite scented climbing roses, such as 'Gloire de Dijon' and its kindred, or the deep red 'Guinée'. Add a jasmine and some night scented stocks, say, for a border of exquisite perfume to drift in through your open windows by day and night.

In mixed borders the newer shrub roses, the hybrid musks and the like, can add their perfume as the old roses do in their season. Repeat-flowering shrub roses – the hybrid musks are often especially showy in autumn – extend the season of a border and give scope for countless lovely combinations of colour, perfume and form.

Within the garden you may need a dividing hedge, perhaps between flower garden and vegetables. What better than a fragrant barrier of *Rosa rugosa*, not only scenting the air around but contributing equally, with its big hips full of vitamin C, to our sense of taste, if we care to use its bounty in rosehip jam or syrup. A few petals of *Rosa rugosa* in a cup of China tea give it a delicious fragrance and taste, too. For a taller hedge the sweet briar, *Rosa rubiginosa*, or one of its hybrid offspring, known, collectively as the Penzance briers, would be suitable.

Perhaps the message is, think of your roses – whether old or new – as scented climbers or shrubs, not as 'roses' in a separate category, to be segregated in the garden. The Queen of Flowers deserves better than a ghetto to grow in.

PART III
HIGH SUMMER

5
TREES, SHRUBS AND FLOWERS

TREES

For their fragrance, as much as their beauty, magnolias again dominate the garden in high summer. *Magnolia grandiflora*, the great evergreen tree of the south-eastern United States, gives us its big, creamy white flowers over a long season and freely diffuses its rich lemony scent on the air. Its hybrid with the related *Magnolia virginiana* is called 'Maryland', a valuable tree or large shrub which flowers at an early age. Aristocrat of all the evergreen tree magnolias we can grow in this climate is *M. delavayi*. Here we have a tree with huge leaves like a rubber plant's, and fleeting flowers that, examined closely, seem to be fashioned of primrose suede. Their scent is delicious. It does need shelter, or a wall, except for gardens which enjoy the mildest of climates.

By comparison, other scented flowering trees of high summer are hardly in the running. The odour of the fluffy, creamy flowers of the sweet chestnut are not to everyone's taste, nor are those of privet. For all that the tree privet, *Ligustrum lucidum*, is a beautiful thing with great white plumes and shiny dark green leaves.

The eucryphias are sweeter, but their scent is often faint and elusive. Best, probably, are *E. lucida* with leaves white-glaucous beneath, and its hybrid offspring *E. × intermedia* 'Rostrevor'. All the eucryphias have white, bowl-shaped flowers with prominent, often rosy-tipped stamens, rather like a white rose of Sharon. Their upright, columnar habit makes them valuable trees for limited space or to create a vertical accent; but they need sheltered gardens.

SHRUBS

For flower power as well as scent, the high summer shrub garden is dominated by the buddleias. All the forms of *B. davidii* are honey-scented. So, most markedly, is the lovely *B.* 'Lochinch', with its grey foliage and big spikes of lavender blue, orange-eyed flowers. Like the variegated philadelphus, this is a plant to site where you can see it glow, at dusk, seemingly infused with its own moonlight. Its parent, *B. fallowiana*, with grey-silver foliage and lavender flowers, and the exquisite white variety 'Alba', are also fragrant.

Hebes have spikes of flower, too, though longer and slimmer, often, than the buddleias. One of the most fragrant is the long-tasselled 'Midsummer Beauty', which despite its name seems willing to flower at almost any season. Many others, though, are also sweetly scented, especially the bedding types with bright flowers, derived from *Hebe speciosa*. Spike-flowered again, but needing quite different conditions of peaty soil and ample moisture, are the clethras. Easiest both to grow and to obtain is *C. alnifolia*, best in its long-spiked form 'Paniculata' or pink-flushed

Many Pinks are clove-scented; they are ideally suited to growing in dry stone walls

Lilium regale is a powerfully fragrant and easy lily for border settings, here with *Artemisia* 'Powis Castle'

'Rosea'; the type is creamy white. All clethras are worth seeking out, though *C. arborea* is only for the very mildest areas. Finest of all in flower is *C. delavayi*, which is scarce but sometimes available; its large white lily-of-the-valley flowers have black anthers.

Back into the sun again, we can grow the common myrtle, *Myrtus communis*, for its lovely fragrant puffs of creamy white flowers. Also sweet-scented is *M. luma*, best grown in mild areas where it will make a small tree displaying its cinnamon-barked trunk.

The Californian tree poppies, *Romneya coulteri* and *R. trichocalyx*, are beautiful with their huge papery golden-hearted white flowers and glaucous foliage. They are sweet-scented, though a little too close to cheap scented soap for my taste.

Though *Abelia × grandiflora* is a justly popular shrub offered in many garden centres, you rarely see *A. chinensis*, with smaller, but abundant, pinky white flowers. This is a pity, for it is very fragrant.

CLIMBERS

At this season the trachelospermums flower, beautiful evergreen climbers with shiny foliage and jasmine-like, sweetly fragrant flowers. *T. jasminoides* has the larger leaves, beautifully marked with pink and cream in the hardier variety 'Variegatum', and white flowers ageing to cream. Smaller-leaved *T. asiaticum* has creamy flowers turning to buff or almost apricot.

BORDER PLANTS

One of the most characteristic perfumes of the summer border is the heavy, peppery aroma of the phloxes. All the border phloxes are fragrant, but I want to pick out a few that are less well known, and well worth your seeking out. These are the forms of *P. maculata*, 'Alpha' in lilac-pink and 'Omega' in white with a lilac eye; and the tall spired *P. paniculata* in white, pale lilac or rosy mauve. From this one derived the named border phloxes in all their variety of size and colour. Their fragrance is more marked at evening.

Phlox paniculata

Most clematis are climbers, but a few are herbaceous. Of these the forms of *C. heracleifolia*, with blue hyacinth-like flowers, are very fragrant. Some even lean to the powerful scent of hair-oil! Named kinds, all lovely, are 'Côte d'Azur', 'Campanile' and 'Crépuscule' from France, and the newer, English-raised 'Wyevale' which is the brightest of all.

There are still lilies to be had in high summer, of course, and the flowers of the lily-like crinums are also fragrant. All have widely flared trumpets, white or pink, and long strap-like leaves. Most readily available is *C. × powellii*, in rich pink or white.

Less like lilies to look at, but more closely related to true lilies than the crinums, are hostas. Most are grown solely for their beautiful foliage, with flowers an unimportant extra. Exceptionally, the white flowers of 'Royal Standard' and 'Honeybells', and of their parent *H. plantaginea grandiflora*, are sweetly fragrant.

Less familiar than the bedding verbenas is the tall, spikily airy *V. bonariensis* with an almost endless succession of its small heads of rich purple flowers on branching stems, that glow richly at dusk. They are sweetly scented, and worth having at the front of the border to bring their perfume to the nose; despite their height they are so little leafy that they do not obscure plants behind them. They look magnificent against a backdrop of hydrangeas.

I have saved until last the most exciting of all high summer flowers. For long it was rare and expensive, but now thanks to modern propagation techniques *Cosmos atrosanguineus* can be widely bought and can, indeed should, be grown in every garden. Here is a plant very like a particularly elegant, neat-leaved single dahlia, coloured a rich maroon-chocolate, and smelling exactly like a cup of thick, hot cocoa. Its perfume has quickly earned it the nickname 'chocolate plant.'

ANNUALS AND BIENNIALS

Many annuals and biennials fill the air with scent. A tell-tale name is 'sweet' – sweet alyssum, sweet peas, sweet williams ... But there are plenty of fragrant annuals that have not acquired this pet name.

At the same lowly level as sweet alyssum, *A. maritimum*, with its white, violet or lilac honey-scented flowers, are other easy, hardy annuals such as candytuft, *Iberis odorata*. The blue woodruff, *Asperula azurea setosa*, is another annual of modest size that gives off a delicious perfume.

For rich soils in light shade, suitable annuals are the poached egg flower, *Limnanthes douglasii* – a great bee plant, this – and the little lilac and white *Ionopsidium acaule* with its warm honey scent.

Mignonette, which the French call by its botanical name of *Reseda odorata*, is a hardy annual that, despite its insignificant colouring, is much loved for its sweet scent. This, too, will happily grow in a moist spot in half shade.

Annuals such as these are a delight tucked in around seats. An uncommon little white-flowered annual is the fringe-petalled *Schizopetalum walkeri*, fragrant at all times and especially in the evening, as are the ever-popular petunias. These, of course, are half-hardy, and I want to consider more of the easy, hardy annuals before we meet the trickier creatures that need starting off in heat.

Most stocks are treated as biennials, but the lowly Virginian stock, with its long season of crimson, rose, lilac or white flowers, is raised as a hardy annual. It gives most generously of its perfume after rain.

Sweet sultan is *Centaurea moschata*, its name both in English and Latin suggesting its fragrance. It bears thistle-like flowers in lilac, purple, white or yellow, and needs a rich soil and a sunny position.

Other taller annuals are the annual lupins, the balsams and nasturtiums – though these, of course, also come in dwarf varieties. The Gleam strain is especially well perfumed. Lupins come in many colours, blue *L. hartwegii*, yellow *L. luteus* and the many-toned *L. mutabilis*, all with the scent of a bean-field.

In mild gardens the tobacco flowers may go on from year to year, self-sowing or surviving from the roots, but they are generally treated as half-hardy annuals and planted out after the last frosts. Modern strains with brighter coloured flowers that stay open all day have

Sweet-pea-scented climbing rose 'Madame Gregoire Staechelin' has sumptuous pink flowers in summer

Tobacco flowers and petunias both smell sweetest at night

lost some of their scent but the older kinds, opening only at evening and white or greenish in flower, are powerfully scented. Look out for *Nicotiana alata* 'Grandiflora' in particular if you prefer perfume to bright colours.

In the same family, Solanaceae – the potato family – are the great daturas. Those that can be raised as half-hardy annuals include the yellow *D. chlorantha* (which has a double-flowered form of extreme sweetness), white, violet-flushed *D. fastuosa* and its double white form, and the white and violet *D. meteloides*. All are handsome as well as fragrant, with big trumpet-shaped flowers most sweetly scented at night.

Of the stocks that are treated as half-hardy annuals, both the ten-week stocks and the lovely Nice stocks are deliciously clove-scented. Their colours range from rose, crimson and purple to lilac, pink and white, and a charming soft yellow.

As with tobacco flowers, so with heliotrope. Most of the modern seed strains that have been selected for deep purple colouring have lost much of their scent in the 'improvement'. Old kinds, which were less bold in colour but infinitely sweeter to the nose, were raised from cuttings each year. Where, now, can we find such varieties as 'Lord Roberts' with their almondy fragrance from which they gained the nickname Cherry Pie?

The Brompton stocks are treated as biennials, but they have the same delicious perfume as the annual kinds, and are doubly welcome as they open the season of the stocks in spring. Also biennial are the spicy-scented sweet williams, so well loved for their rich colouring as well as for their perfume. *Scabiosa atropurpurea*, in the deep purple that gave it its specific name, and also in crimson, mauve, lilac, pink or white, is delightfully honey-scented.

But of course the peak of summer fragrance from annuals comes from the sweet peas – or should. But here again, in the search for a wider range of colours, larger, frillier flowers, and a range of heights from the tallest climbing kinds to the little Knee-Hi strains, some of the scent has been lost. If you seek the richest and most delectable scent from your sweet peas, seek out and grow the old kinds such as 'Matucana' and 'Quito' with their small but intensely coloured flowers in maroon and purple, or the paler pink and white 'Painted Lady'. At least one seedsman is offering these and other old kinds, saved and sown lovingly year after year by those to whom fragrance is more precious than fashion.

6

AROMATIC PLANTS

So far we have been considering mainly floral perfumes. The aroma of leaves, and to a lesser extent of bark, wood or fruits, also has an important part to play in the fragrant garden. Many leaves need to be stroked, some even crushed or bruised, before they release their characteristic fragrance, so the sense of touch is brought into play as well, contributing to a fuller sensory experience.

Perhaps the first category of aromatic-leaved plants we think of is herbs. Increasingly popular in cookery, valued by many for their medicinal properties, they are often very beautiful as well.

HERBS

Herb gardens are popular, whether large enough to be enclosed in hedges or small enough to fit in between the spokes of an old cartwheel (the 'wheel of herbs' idea that is easier to plant up than, subsequently, to control!). Even in quite a small space you can make a charming feature of a knot garden, intricately shaped beds picked out in clipped box or santolina hedges and filled with a tapestry of herbs. But this, too, is time-consuming. If it is to look good it must be immaculate, and many herbs are simply too energetic in growth for neat little beds.

An alternative is to choose the most ornamental varieties of herbs and grow them among your other garden plants. Try purple-leaved sage under pink roses or beside creamy brooms; it is a charming shade of grey-purple, not the hard maroon of purple berberis, say, or the purple *Cotinus*. In shadier beds among shrubs the white-variegated apple mint grows well and makes a

palatable, if pallid, mint sauce. Giant chives taste as good as the ordinary kind and are decorative for the front of a flower border. Gold and silver variegated thymes taste as good as the green kinds, golden marjoram too, and bronze fennel is as delicious with fish as the plain green type. With its fox tail plumes of bronze-purple young growth it is a very attractive contrast to pinks and purples, or among yellow and white flowers. Even parsley, if you choose the tightly curled kinds (admittedly they have less flavour than the plain-leaved) is handsome enough to use with flowers. And you can bed out the strikingly black-purple form of basil for a fine foliage contrast as well as the best herb to use on a tomato salad.

PLANTS TO WALK ON

Those who open their gardens to the public, or who have rumbustious small children, spend much of their time hoping their plants won't be trampled. But some plants reward us when we tread on them, by releasing their aromatic essence into the air around us. The place to grow such plants is among paving – patio or path – or around a seat, anywhere where we can tread lightly; for if we abuse them they will turn to crushed brown mats. For sunny places chamomile, *Anthemis nobilis*, is first choice for its concentrated apple aroma. The most suitable variety to form a low, mossy green mat is the non-flowering 'Treneague'. The lower-growing thymes, too, enjoy full sun. Forms of *Thymus serpyllum* form a close mat and come in different colours, with flowers of purple or pink, white, crimson or lilac; *T. serpyllum lanuginosus* has pretty pale flowers among

Old-fashioned sweet peas, like 'Painted Lady', often have even more scent than the modern varieties

Purple sage, ginger mint and rue – three aromatic and ornamental herbs growing in close and colourful association

furry grey foliage. The caraway thyme, *T. herba-barona*, got its botanical name from its old use to flavour barons of beef; when bruised it does, indeed, smell just like caraway.

For shadier spots, a pair of mints are ideal. Pennyroyal, *Mentha pulegium*, is the larger in leaf and flower, putting up little spikes of mauve-purple over mats of dark green leaves. Even more pungent is the tiny *Mentha requienii*, growing close to the ground with tight-packed, tiny bright green leaves among which the minute mauve flowers appear in summer.

SILVER- AND GREY-LEAVED PLANTS

Not all aromatic plants, of course, count as herbs. Of several silver-leaved plants that are deliciously or pungently aromatic, only lavender perhaps comes instantly into the category 'herb' in our minds. As well as the common lavender, and the darker-flowered, dwarfer kinds such as 'Hidcote', try the French lavender, *Lavandula stoechas*, for its silvery leaves and cockaded purple flowers. Of the common lavenders the old English Lavender, *L. spica*, with its broad grey leaves and tall spikes of pale flowers, has the best perfume and makes a handsome bush.

Salvia lavandulifolia is a sage with narrower, greyer leaves than the common culinary sage; its botanical name indicates a (rather remote) similarity to lavender. To my taste it is not quite right in sage and onion stuffing; but as an ornamental plant it is first-rate. The curry plant, varieties of *Helichrysum*, is definitely not for cooking despite its name. It earns it from the spicy scent, like cheap curry powder, given off by its narrow silver leaves. Names to look out for are *H. italicum*, *H. serotinum*, *H. fontanesii*. Like many aromatic plants, many of which are native of hotter countries than ours, they release their aroma more freely on hot days.

As well as lavender itself, there are two other delightful blue-mauve flowered shrubs that are pleasantly aromatic. *Caryopteris* × *clandonensis* has narrow grey leaves with a sharp fresh scent, and fluffy heads of blue

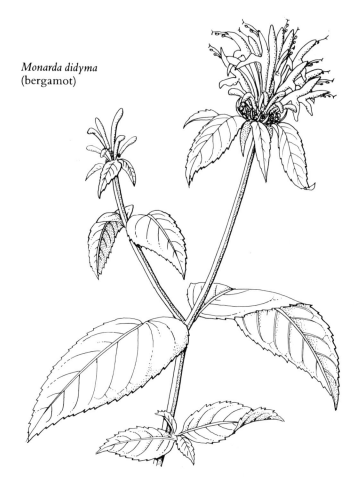

Monarda didyma (bergamot)

flowers in late summer. More turpentine-like in aroma are the Russian sages, *Perovskia atriplicifolia* and its form 'Blue Spire' with dissected leaves and long, lovely spires of furry blue flowers on white stems. Do not be misled by the common name; these are not true sages.

The cotton lavenders – which are not lavenders – are forms of *Santolina*. All have bobble-like flowers, some bright yellow, some primrose or cream. *S. incana* is the common, bright silver kind with tight foliage and vivid flowers; it has a good little dwarf kind 'Nana'. Nicer, I think, is *S. neapolitana* with more feathery foliage and lemon yellow flowers, or 'Sulphurea' with paler flowers, easier to fit into colour schemes. Pale yellows are precious, cooling hot schemes of reds and oranges or contrasting quietly with blues and mauves.

Several artemisias are silvery-leaved. Look for 'Lambrook Silver' with finely cut foliage, or the newer 'Powis Castle'. This one has the advantage of never flowering, so keeping its neat outline all year.

Much less familiar are the daisy bushes, *Olearia*. Of these, the uncommon *O. ilicifolia* with narrow, toothed, grey-green leaves, *O. mollis* with grey foliage and greyish *O. moschata* have all somewhat musk-scented leaves. All are good shrubs for milder gardens.

AROMATIC HERBACEOUS PLANTS

Bergamot, *Monarda didyma*, is an ornamental border plant that has whorls of scarlet-crimson, pink, purple or magenta flowers in summer, above mats of aromatic foliage which, when you bruise it, smells like a freshly-opened packet of Earl Grey tea. Bergamot, indeed, has the alternative name of Oswego Tea, for it can be used to brew an aromatic cup.

Oil of geranium is extracted from a true geranium, not a pelargonium, though – as we shall see – many of these latter are very aromatic. *Geranium macrorrhizum* has sharply pungent foliage forming good ground cover, and quite showy flowers of magenta, pink or white in early summer.

Just as Russian sage is not a sage, and cotton lavender not a lavender, so is catmint not a mint. *Nepeta cataria* is the real catmint, but the name is also given to others, such as the familiar blue-mauve, grey-leaved *Nepeta × faassenii* which assorts so well with roses. In the absence of the real thing, cats will happily roll about in this one, too, and spoil its outline.

With a name that at first glance looks rather like a Latinized version of catmint (but there is no connection) is *Calamintha*. Two species are found in gardens: the pink to magenta *C. grandiflora* and the smaller flowered *C. nepetoides*, which has pale milky mauve

flowers. Both have a sharp aroma, released when the leaves are bruised, reminiscent of mint; the second especially is much visited by bees.

A plant that has seen an increase in popularity lately, since the introduction of its vividly variegated form with magenta-pink and cream markings on dark green, is *Houttuynia cordata*. A vigorous spreader in moist conditions, but restrained in dry sun, this is a plant with white flowers, cone-shaped in the double-flowered kind. The heart-shaped leaves have a pungent smell not enjoyed by all, but which to me are reminiscent of oranges – not the pulp, but the tangier smell of the peel.

MEDITERRANEANS AND OTHERS

The hillsides of the Mediterranean are aromatic with countless fragrant herbs, origanum and rosemary,

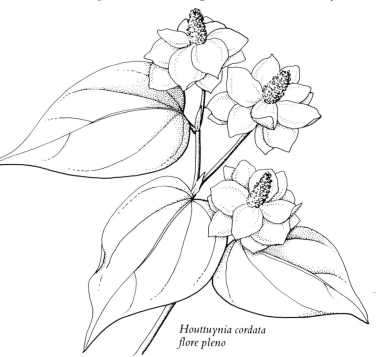

Houttuynia cordata flore pleno

Caryopteris x clandonensis has sharply aromatic foliage and blue flowers in summer; here *Allium pulchellum* has seeded among its stems

Olearia ilicifolia has attractive, musk-scented foliage toothed like holly

myrtle and bay, lavender and many of the great tribe of sun roses. These belong in the cistus family and their leaves exude a resinous, aromatic gum. *Cistus ladanifer* is, indeed, called the gum cistus because of this quality. It is also beautiful in flower, with white papery blooms. It is not one of the hardier cistus, though. If you garden in a cold area you would do better with the hybrid *C. × cyprius*, its white flowers marked with the same basal blotch of chocolate-maroon as its parent the gum cistus. Another child of the gum cistus is *C. × aguilari* with white flowers, unblotched, and crinkly green resinous leaves.

One of the most beautiful of all is *C. palhinhae* from Portugal, with shiny, sticky leaves and huge papery white flowers. If you like your cistus to come in magenta-purple, go for *C. × purpureus* which joins the rich pink colouring of one parent with the chocolate basal blotch of the other, the gum cistus again.

The Mediterranean does not have a monopoly of aromatic-leaved plants. From California comes the uncommon *Umbellularia californica*, allied to bay and quite like it to look at, but more pungently aromatic, with an almost medicinal smell that is said, in too great a dose, to induce headaches. To me it smells more like something that would clear a head!

From Mexico, too, come some good aromatics, including some of the shrubby, rather tender sages. *Salvia neurepia* has scarlet flowers and green leaves that smell like pineapple and perspiration. Pineapple alone is the unmistakable scent of the leaves of another red-flowered sage, *Salvia rutilans*.

TREES AND SHRUBS

The orange family includes some aromatic-leaved shrubs. I have already mentioned the Mexican orange, *Choysia ternata*. More pungent than this is rue, *Ruta graveolens*; best in its blue-leaved variety 'Jackman's Blue'. Mix it with silver and grey-leaved shrubs for a beautiful effect in hot, dry soils. Another shrub, of quite a different family, that adds another tone of soft grey-blue to such a colour-scheme is *Hebe cupressoides*. Its name means 'cypress-like', and it is indeed much more like a dwarf conifer than the shrubby veronica that it is. It not only looks like a conifer – it also smells exactly like a pencil cedar. Next time you sharpen a pencil, sniff the shavings; that's exactly what this hebe smells like. It has little pale blue flowers in summer.

Eucalyptus, of course, is an unmistakable smell reminiscent of childhood colds. We can recapture it in the garden by planting one of the hardier kinds. *E. gunnii* with circular blue-grey juvenile leaves is the best known and is easily obtained. More handsome by far is *E. niphophila*, with sickle-shaped leaves and beautiful bark marbled white, cream, grey, green and buff.

Of deciduous trees, walnuts and some poplars are aromatic in leaf. The balsam poplars, *Populus balsamifera* and others, sometimes give off great wafts of scent; at other times they keep it to themselves. The handsomely variegated *P. × candicans* 'Aurora' is usually chosen for the flower-like effect of its white, pink and green leaves, but these too are balsam-scented.

Several aromatic shrubs have already had a mention. One that cannot be overlooked is lemon verbena, *Aloysia triphylla* (also, more descriptively, known as *Lippia citriodora*). Nor can I fail to mention some of the aromatic rhododendrons, such as *R. glaucophyllum* with leaves white beneath, smelling powerfully of saddle soap and supple leather. The blue-leaved Cinnabarina series with their beautiful waxy bells are also aromatic.

Bark, wood and gum

Gum trees, eucalyptuses and gum cistus have had their mention. Conifer bark, too, is resinous and aromatic, sometimes turpentine-like. The rather tender evergreen *Drimys winteri* has fragrant bark, and the smaller *D. aromatica* is not so named for nothing. The bark of *Magnolia salicifolia* smells of lemon, or of anise.

Camphor wood comes from *Cinnamomum camphora*, which can be grown in mild gardens in Britain. *Calycanthus* and the related *Chimonanthus* which flowers in winter are aromatic throughout – leaves, wood, flowers, seeds. Of herbaceous plants with aromatic roots there are *Sedum rhodiola*, the rose root, and *Inula helenium* with roots that smell of bananas.

SCENTS OF EVENING AND NIGHT

Several of the plants already mentioned are especially fragrant at night. Such are the honeysuckles, the lemon day lily *Hemerocallis citrina*, and mignonette, which despite its French-sounding name is known in France by its botanical name, *Reseda*. Sweet rocket, too, is more fragrant at night.

Quite early in the year, in spring, the evenings are filled with the penetrating sweetness of our native *Daphne laureola*, and of the far finer *D. pontica*. These evergreen shrubs have yellow-green flowers; the second has broad, glossy green foliage and makes an ideal plant for a shady corner by a door or window where you will often pass at night.

Night-scented flowers are not necessarily very attractive. The night-scented stock, *Matthiola bicornis* (*M. tristis*) has dull little flowers of muddy lilac or whitish-brown, but its evening fragrance is unmatched. The plants are slender enough to sow among other, showier flowers. If you can contrive to plant them beneath a window which, in summer, you have open in all suitable weathers, their perfume will fill the room as well as the garden.

Handsomer in flower are the tobacco plants. I have already recommended *N. alata* 'Grandiflora'; the perfume of its green-backed white trumpets is especially strong at night.

In the same family, Solanaceae (which also includes the humble potato), is the spectacular *Datura suaveolens*, a large, tender shrub with magnificent white trumpets, diffusing a powerful sweet scent, especially at night. Related to the datura again, but much hardier, is *Cestrum parqui*. A shrub which, in colder areas, behaves like a herbaceous perennial, springing up from ground level, this has sprays of yellow flowers in summer, and at night –

Datura suaveolens

From the leaves of *Geranium macrorrhizum* Oil of Geranium is distilled. Here the white-flowered form
makes dense cover among shrubs

from early bedtime on – is very sweetly scented.

The marvel of Peru, *Mirabilis jalapa*, is also sometimes called the four o'clock plant because its flowers do not begin to open until late afternoon. By evening they are well open and emitting their rich perfume.

The name evening primrose describes another flower that opens late in the day. *Oenothera biennis* is a biennial with a long flowering season. Its sweetly-scented blooms open suddenly ...

... the marvel of Peru, its rose-pink flowers ... flowers a little like those of a verbena and are honey-scented, especially at night. *Abronia arenaria*, the Californian sand verbena, has yellow flowers and a scent reminiscent of honeysuckle.

Mention pelargoniums and scent in the same breath, and the scented-leaved kinds come to mind. Two species, however, have fragrant flowers most notable at night. *Pelargonium triste* is so named because the sad, browny-green colouring of its flowers ... their perfume is unique. The ... pelargonium is so called due to the smallness of ... greenish ... flowers are also ... through its ...

... if one could afford a conservatory ... evergreen magnolia, but it ... a small ... shrub than a large tree, and its evening white-flowered ... are particularly sweet at night. How lovely to be able to stroll into the conservatory after dinner on summer evenings and inhale the perfume of something so exotic! In addition, I would also be tempted to grow the exquisite *Gladiolus tristis*, with gentle yellow flowers open all day but emitting their delicious scent only at night.

PART IV

AUTUMN/WINTER PLANTS
AND PLANTS UNDER COVER
8
AUTUMN

TREES AND SHRUBS

By autumn, flowering trees and shrubs are fewer, and those that flowered earlier in the year are setting fruit. *Magnolia grandiflora* continues to produce a few of its perfumed flowers until well into autumn, and the hebes are still performing.

Belonging entirely to this season are the clerodendrums. *C. trichotomum*, and its less appealing variant *C. trichotomum fargesii*, were nicknamed the Aston Villa trees by a friend of mine, after their coloured fruits: thick maroon calyces holding bright turquoise berries. It is the flowers that are fragrant, however, in late summer and autumn, white-petalled and set off by the same red calyces. Do not bruise the leaves of clerodendrums: they smell of burnt rubber.

Even more rubbery in leaf-smell, and just as fragrant in flower as the tree-like *Clerodendrum trichotomum* is the shrubby *C. bungei*. Though smelly, it is handsome in leaf, and bears striking large heads of rich rosy pink scented flowers. In cold areas it may die to ground level, like many other less hardy shrubs, and with spring bob up again as though it were a herbaceous plant.

The last of the privets, the elegant *Ligustrum quihoui*, produces its great white sprays in early autumn, and the abelias will still be in flower.

The inconspicuous white flowers of *Osmanthus heterophyllus* (syn. *aquifolium*) appear in autumn, betraying their presence by their sweet smell. By late autumn it is the time of *Camellia sasanqua* and its variants in white, pink or crimson, all with a sweet scent.

For mild climates only is *Eupatorium weinmannianum* (syn. *micranthum*), with tiny pinky white heads giving off a curious scent, acrid and yet agreeable.

LINGERING FLOWERS OF SUMMER

Among the typical sights of autumn, the chrysanthemums and blackened dahlias, there are still echoes of summer. The last of the phloxes are in flower, late lilies, and some roses. Notable among these are the hybrid musks, which often produce a magnificent second crop of flower in autumn.

With their propensity to be slaughtered by frost, dahlias belong perhaps more exactly to late summer than to autumn. Their strange sharp scent is very characteristic and evocative. Even more pungent, and – in the garden at least – typically autumnal, is the smell of chrysanthemums. It seems a shame that chrysanthemums can now be had in a pot all year round; no longer do we wait with mingled pleasure and apprehension for their season, that heralds the onset of winter. But the hardy and pretty Korean chrysanthemums are still worth growing in the garden for their late flowers and rich range of colours.

FLOWERS IN AUTUMN

In autumn flower some very beautiful bulbous plants needing warmth to succeed. The large pink trumpets of *Amaryllis belladonna* (syn. *Brunsvigia rosea*) are deliciously scented like ripe apricots and appear on dark stems, unaccompanied by leaves. A mass of these takes years to achieve, but is well worth waiting for.

Also for warm gardens are the hardy gingers, species of *Hedychium*. Only a few are available commercially, but for fragrance it is hard to beat one of the least uncommon, *H. gardnerianum*. This is a most beautiful plant with blade-like leaves and open, cylindrical spires of rich yellow, or pale primrose, exquisitely scented flowers.

The familiar highly bred, brightly coloured gladioli are unscented, but several wild species gladioli and their near hybrids are fragrant. Some have received mention for their perfume at night – *G. tristis* and others. Here, for autumn, I must mention *Gladiolus callianthus*, more familiar under the name *Acidanthera bicolor*. 'Bicolor' describes its lovely flowers, pure white with maroon blotches in the throat. They are delightfully fragrant.

FALLEN LEAVES

Some fallen leaves have their own very characteristic smell, distinct from the general autumn aroma that pervades the garden. Strawberry leaves are said to have a special perfume when dying, but it is extremely elusive and I am not sure I have ever caught it. Walnut leaves, always aromatic, are more so in death. But the most powerful scent from fallen leaves comes from the coin-shaped foliage, golden in decay, of the beautiful tree called *Cercidiphyllum japonicum*. Once fallen, and for just a few days, they smell exactly like hot burnt toffee, and this tempting aroma carries on the air for quite some distance.

FRUIT

Many fruits are more or less aromatic as well as tasty. None is more so than the yellow quinces produced by many 'japonicas' or flowering quinces, forms of *Chaenomeles*. When you plant one for its bright, early flowers in red, orange or salmon, pink or white, remember its bright yellow fruits, which combine, visually, to perfection with the tiny scarlet berries of the fishbone cotoneaster, *C. horizontalis*. Pick a few quinces for the house; in a bowl in a warm room they will give generously of their spicy aroma. You can also make a delicious quince jelly from them.

Acidanthera bicolor

Cistus palhinhae releases its resinous aroma most freely in hot weather and needs full sun in Britain

Cestrum parqui is a half-shrubby border plant, very fragrant at night

9

WINTER

The garden in winter is a subject in itself, and some beautiful books have been written which would tempt even the most determined fair-weather gardener outside in the cold. Here, of course, I want to consider only scented flowers for winter.

Happily, there are some of the sweetest scents of the year to be enjoyed in winter. Because evergreens are so valuable in the winter garden, let's look at the precious shrubs that not only keep their leaves in winter, but also bring fragrance with their flowers.

Of these, none can beat the daphnes. A fairly newly introduced daphne goes by the perplexing name of *D. bholua* (try saying 'bo-LOO-ah') and comes in evergreen and deciduous forms. The evergreen kinds were collected at lower altitudes in the Himalayas and are thus less hardy, but well worth trying in a sheltered corner for their exquisite scent. Smaller and much tougher is little creeping *D. blagayana*, with heads of creamy fragrant flowers.

Easiest is *Daphne odora* 'Aureomarginata', a low, rounded shrub with a penetrating sweetness to its white and mauve-pink flowers. The leaves are margined with a thin line of gold.

Of similar size, but with much narrower leaves than the daphnes, are the sarcococcas. Their flowers are scarcely showy – little bunches of narrow, dingy white or pinkish petals – but their sweet honey scent carries for yards around. *Sarcococca hookeriana digyna* is perhaps the best, but others worth growing are *S. humilis* and the taller *S. ruscifolia*.

Against a wall, in all but the warmest gardens, you could grow *Azara microphylla* with its neat shining dark green foliage and, nestling modestly on the underside of the sprays of foliage, tiny yellow flowers.

These smell of vanilla – indeed, they have exactly the smell of custard powder. For an even warmer corner you could choose *Acacia dealbata*, the florists' mimosa, so handsome with its blue-green, ferny foliage and fluffy yellow bobbles of flower that smell a little like violets. It is so easy from seed that I urge anyone with a warm corner to try it.

These sheltered corners do have many rivals for their space, it's true. There are those two sweetly scented, evergreen-leaved buddleias: *B. asiatica* with long creamy tassels and *B. auriculata* with shorter creamy buff flower heads. The yellow, pea-flowered *Coronilla glauca* and dwarfer *C. valentina* flower at almost any season of the year, but commonly in winter, and have a delicious warm scent.

If you have room, both *Elaeagnus pungens* (brightest in the gold-variegated form 'Maculata') and larger-leaved *E. macrophylla* are handsome foliage plants with the bonus of discreet, but very fragrant, flowers. Both the flowers and the underside of the leaves have a silvery scurfy covering.

King of the evergreen winter shrubs for flower scent is *Mahonia japonica*, with arching sprays of yellow flowers shaped like, and smelling like, lily-of-the-valley. Beware of imitations; some of the newer hybrids, such as 'Charity', though striking in flower, do not have the exquisite perfume.

DECIDUOUS SHRUBS

The evergreen shrubs have many rivals in fragrance among the choice band of deciduous shrubs flowering in winter. Daphnes are again represented, by *D.*

mezereum, so charming when wreathed in its purplish pink or white flowers.

The wintersweet, *Chimonanthus praecox*, is aptly named. To my nose this has the most exquisite of all winter perfumes, and a sprig or two will fill a room with scent. The shrub itself is no beauty and takes seven years or so to flower; but when you inhale the spicy sweetness of those little waxy, almost colourless flowers you will forgive it everything. Choose, if you can obtain it, the yellow-flowered variety 'Luteus', just as fragrant but more striking in flower.

Witch hazels are known for their scent, though not all varieties have enough of that spicy, sharp perfume. The common *Hamamelis mollis* has it, and the more beautiful variety 'Pallida' with the unusual spidery flowers in a delightful shade of pale lemon yellow. *H. japonica* 'Zuccariniana' flowers later than most and its sharp, almost rough scent is unmistakable. Most of the red-flowered kinds are short on perfume, but *H. japonica flavopurpurascens* is fragrant, and so is the coppery red 'Feuerzauber' ('Magic Fire').

The shrubby, winter-flowering honeysuckles run the wintersweet close for perfume. Don't expect flowers as showy as the climbing honeysuckles. These have little creamy flowers in pairs. Look for *Lonicera fragrantissima*, *L. standishii* or, best of all, the hybrid *L. × purpusii* with slightly larger flowers.

From the winter-flowering viburnums you can expect a powerful, carrying scent reminiscent of almonds. *V. fragrans* is now correctly, if less descriptively, called *V. farreri* and has heads of pink-budded, white flowers; or pure white in the form *candidissimum*. The name of *V. foetens* seems to imply an unpleasant smell, but it is actually agreeably scented. Equally uncommon is *V. grandiflorum* (syn. *V. nervosum*) with larger flowers. Crossed with *V. farreri* it produced the hybrid *V. × bodnantense*, which has gained immense and justifiable popularity for its sweet almondy scent and pink-white flowers. 'Dawn' is the pinker form, 'Deben' nearer to white.

BULBS AND HERBACEOUS PLANTS

Among such riches of shrubs for winter fragrance, the little plants don't get much of a look in. Snowdrops are fragrant, however, some more than others but all sweet, if sometimes rather faint. The related snowflakes, *Leucojum vernum*, smell rather like violets. *Crocus imperati* is a winter-flowering crocus with a perfume, and *Iris reticulata* is scented, too. It can't compare, however, with the true winter-flowering iris, *I. unguicularis* (which used to bear the prettier name of *I. stylosa*). Quite large flowers of exquisite clear mauve, white, or purple are delightfully fragrant. Pick them in bud and watch them unfurl from scrolled, buff-backed buds when brought into a warm room.

With winter flowers especially, it is perhaps nicest to enjoy them indoors, in little posies. In the garden you can, of course, construct a special winter garden, or winter border, if you have space. But I think the nicest way with these sweet-scented flowers of winter is to plant them where you pass often, by a front or back door or wherever, so you enjoy their perfume whenever you go by.

Lonicera × purpusii

Gladiolus tristis deserves to be grown far more often for its dainty flowers and exquisite evening perfume

The Belladonna Lily, *Amaryllis belladonna*, smells of ripe apricots. It flowers best when well baked by the sun.

10

GREENHOUSE AND CONSERVATORY PLANTS

If not many of us can afford one of those grand and beautiful conservatories attached to a gracious house of mellow brick or warm stone, a great many gardeners now have a small greenhouse, perhaps as a lean-to to the house, forming a garden room, or at the very least a light and airy porch. We can grow fragrant plants here as well as in the garden and, of course, indoors.

SHRUBS

If I were limited to just one fragrant shrub for a warm greenhouse, it would have to be a gardenia. There are many species, all with white or creamy flowers, but for the heady sweetness of its perfume none can yield to the double-flowered *Gardenia jasminoides*, its lovely blooms set off by shiny dark foliage.

For a cooler house, no more than frost-free, the choice is wide. *Acacia baileyana*, with steel-blue feathery foliage, bears its violet-scented yellow bobbles in winter. At much the same season come the buff-yellow, sweetly fragrant flowers, borne in sprays among slender leaves, of the South African *Freylinia lanceolata*.

The florists' broom, *Genista fragrans*, bears its fragrant yellow broom-flowers over a long season in late winter and early spring. For fragrant or aromatic leaves in a cool house you could grow the Australian mint bushes, *Prostanthera*, with their pretty flowers in lilac, pink or white. Like the genista and lemon verbena (*Aloysia triphylla*) and, indeed, the acacia, they will grow outside in warm, sheltered gardens. Lemon verbena is so powerfully and sweetly lemon-scented that whether grown indoors or out it must be some-where you pass often, to touch it and release its perfume.

Heliotrope is often now grown from seed as any other bedding plants, but the old named kinds, if you can trace them, are much more fragrant. How sad that, as with sweet peas and many other old, scented favourites, fragrance has in too many varieties been sacrificed to depth or brightness of colour.

In a cool house you can grow your own lemons; the variety 'Meyer's' is the one to choose. It bears at all seasons typical citrus flowers, the true orange blossom, and these are followed by aromatic lemons of good size and copious juice.

CLIMBERS

Of the several delectably fragrant climbers for greenhouse conditions, most are white-flowered. All the tender jasmines with their characteristic perfume are white, at most flushed with pink. The most familiar is *Jasminum polyanthum*; you could also look out for *J. angulare*, *J. azoricum* and the tellingly named *J. suavissimum*, the 'most sweet'.

The elegant waxy white flowers of stephanotis are seen less often now that heating a greenhouse has become so expensive; for this twining plant needs hothouse treatment. The honey-scented hoyas will manage with a little less heat, and are adaptable to room conditions as well. The pink-flushed *H. carnosa* is of climbing habit, the better to display its hanging heads of waxy, incense-fragrant flowers. Blush-white *H. bella* is only semi-climbing.

You would need a big glasshouse for the giant

Hoya carnosa

honeysuckle, *Lonicera hildebrandiana*. It bears flowers up to six inches long, creamy-white ageing to buff yellow, sweetly scented, and the plant is in scale with the flowers.

More manageable in size is the yellow-flowered *Gelsemium sempervirens*, which belongs to the same family as the buddleias – and indeed *Buddleia madagascariensis* could have received mention among the shrubs for its warmly perfumed orange tresses.

The Chilean jasmine, *Mandevilla suaveolens*, is neither a jasmine nor Chilean – it is native of Brazil. For all that it can be grown in warm gardens on a sheltered wall, outside. However, for its flared trumpets, pure white and shaped like a giant periwinkle (to which family it belongs) and its sweet scent it is worth conservatory space in colder areas. It is easy to raise from seed.

A climber with the curious name of *Wattakaka sinensis* used to be hard to obtain, but is now more readily available. It has flowers rather like a hoya, white with a central zone of red spots, and a delightful scent.

Although the plant is pretty hardy, *Clematis cirrhosa balearica* is worth greenhouse space for two reasons: it flowers in winter, so the frail creamy green flowers, speckled like an egg inside, are protected from the weather, and under cover its lemony fragrance is noticeable, which it is not among the buffeting winds of winter.

RHODODENDRONS

A group of beautiful rhododendrons with large, white, lily-like flowers and an intoxicating lily perfume need the protection of a greenhouse. Names to look out for are *Rhododendron johnstoneanum*, the exquisite and rare *R. nuttallii*, *R. bullatum* and *R. edgeworthii*. Addicts will soon discover others. Among named, hybrid kinds are 'Fragrantissimum' and 'Lady Alice Fitzwilliam', and the blush pink 'Countess of Haddington'.

SCENTED-LEAVED GERANIUMS

The scented-leaved geraniums, actually pelargoniums, are justly popular as pot plants for their fragrant leaves. By assembling a collection you can have the aromas of rose (*P. capitatum*, or the variegated 'Lady Plymouth'), of lemon (*P. crispum*, *P. citriodorum*), or of orange ('Prince of Orange'). Peppermint-scented pelargoniums include the woolly-leaved *P. tomentosum*. Some pelargoniums are pine or resin-scented, *P. fragrans* among them. The leaves of *P. quercifolium*, the oak-leaved geranium, emit the scent of incense.

SUCCULENTS

Succulents are not usually grown for their perfume, but who could omit the night-blooming cactus, *Selenicereus grandiflorus*, with its huge white and gold, vanilla-scented flowers that last just one night?

The hardy gingers are for mild gardens or conservatory protection. This is *Hedychium gardnerianum*.

Acidanthera bicolor can be planted out each year like gladioli – it is now called *Gladiolus callianthus* – or grown under cover

BULBS, CORMS AND RHIZOMES

In cold gardens the hardy gingers, described in chapter 8, deserve a place in a frost-free greenhouse for their scent. Much earlier in the year come the highly popular freesias, with their exquisite perfume. Creamy white or primrose yellow *F. refracta* is the most deliciously fragrant, but the coloured hybrids are often almost as good.

The tuberose, *Polianthes tuberosa*, has perhaps the most exotic perfume of any plant we can grow. It has waxy white flowers, double in the variety 'The Pearl' which gains, if that were possible, in the intensity of perfume by developing the extra petals.

Eucharis grandiflora has beautiful white flowers and a rich perfume rather like that of *Lilium regale*. And indeed, many lilies can be grown in pots and brought indoors when in flower, or in the conservatory. As I write a potful of *Lilium speciosum* is filling the room with its sweet heady perfume, while its large star-shaped flowers, rich crimson-pink outlined in white, are enhanced by the coppery-brown pollen on the stamens. The white-flowered *Lilium longiflorum* is sometimes called the Easter lily because its sweetly scented trumpets appear early in the year.

The white-flowered, spidery-petalled *Hymenocallis* are all sweetly scented and worthy of greenhouse space. There is a pale yellow kind, 'Sulphur Queen', and the rarest of rare *H. macrostephana*, with immense white, yellow-throated blooms.

Among all the excitement of discovering that by selection the wild *Cyclamen persicum* could be developed to produce huge flowers in a great range of colours, much or all of the scent of the wildling was lost. Happily a new line in selection is giving us back the fragrance of the original, coupled with smaller, more elegant flowers on neat little plants, often with beautifully marked foliage.

ORCHIDS

Epidendrum fragrans

Many hothouse orchids are fragrant, and their flowers last for a very long time. Among them are the honey-scented *Dendrobium aggregatum* and *D. nobile*, the musky *Coelogyne barbata*, *C. speciosa* and some other dendrobiums, including *D. moschatum* with its telltale name. *Coelogyne cristata* is said to smell of bananas and coconut, and *Cattleya citrina* of limes. Species of *Epidendrum* have a heavy sweet scent likened to carnation or stephanotis, *Odontoglossum pendulum* smells of roses and *O. pulchellum* of lily-of-the-valley. Some *Brassia* species are scented, while *Lycaste aromatica* has a heavy lemon perfume and other species of *Lycaste* remind one of vanilla. So too, of course, does the vanilla orchid itself.

Other orchids that are scented are *Cattleya intermedia* and the sweetly perfumed *Coelogyne massangenana*, *Cymbidium simulans*. *C. ensifolium* and, most of all, *C. eburneum*. Some of the gorgeous Vandas are perfumed too: *Vanda cristata* and *V. tricolor*, and *V. suavis*, with a scent that resembles carnations.

APPENDIX I

FITTING THEM IN

Having read through to this point, I hope by now you are asking yourself how you can grow more of these lovely scented beauties in your garden. Unless you are just starting a new garden, the chances are that like most of us you already have rather too many plants for the available space. I would like to suggest a way in which you can grow more plants without taking in more garden. For new gardeners, this approach – for it is no more than that, not a complicated technique – will not only help you to grow more plants than you thought possible, but will also reduce the amount of work once the plants are established. I call it tenement gardening.

In nature, plants grow in layers – like the storeys of an apartment block, if you will – hence 'tenement'. At the ground floor level are the lowly plants, herbaceous mainly, with some trailing or creeping shrubby plants. Bulbs inhabit the basement. Above the ground level are shrubs, at various heights, with the taller perennials too. The topmost levels are the domaine of trees, small, middling and tall. Adorning these various levels, rather as squatters, are the climbers, infiltrating their stems among the hosts they use as support.

By adopting exactly these principles in your garden you may be able to enjoy four or five times as much value, in beauty and fragrance, from each square yard of soil. You will quickly find that by working with the plants, using nature's methods rather than struggling against them, your plants will grow more freely, the soil will be covered almost everywhere, and you will thus have far fewer weeds to worry about than when you scrupulously kept bare, hoed soil around each plant. Even annuals can be fitted into this scheme of things, popped into any little empty patch of soil, to fill it with informal beauty, instead of bullied into regimented ranks needing constant attention.

You can plan your planting to create the maximum impact, by having everything flower at the same time. Or you can extend the season of flower and fragrance from each corner of your garden by planting for a succession of seasonal effects. Often you can liven up a shrub or tree that is unexciting out of flower, by using it to support a climber that flowers before or after its host. You can waken a summer flower border by planting bulbs between the clumps of hardy perennials, to flower among their freshly emerging spring shoots. You can plant grape hyacinths among your roses, fragrant narcissi in a patch of long grass; scatter seed of night-scented stocks beneath a window which you leave open in summer, or rim a shady border with violets. You could plant a fragrant bower over a garden seat, or a scented shrub by a door where you often pass. Whatever your scheme of things you will be able to add fragrance for all seasons.

The pleasure you get from your garden will be enhanced immeasurably, once you begin to consider fragrance as part of its design; not an accident, but an essential quality. Even weeding becomes a pleasure, when on hands and knees you bring your nose closer to the perfume of your smaller plants.

Gelsemium sempervirens needs glasshouse protection except in mildest areas

Mandevilla suaveolens has brilliantly white flowers all summer in a conservatory or on a sheltered, sunny wall.

APPENDIX II
PLANT LISTS

TREES WITH FRAGRANT FLOWERS

Acacia baileyana
   A. dealbata
Aesculus hippocastanum
Cladrastis lutea
Eucryphia × *intermedia* 'Rostrevor'
   E. lucida
Fraxinus mariesii
   F. ornus
Laburnum alpinum
   L. × *watereri* 'Vossii'
Ligustrum lucidum
Magnolia delavayi
   M. grandiflora
   M. hypoleuca
   M. kobus

M × *loebneri* & cvs
M. salicifolia
M. sprengeri diva
Malus angustifolia
   M. baccata
   M. coronaria 'Charlottae'
   M. floribunda
   M. 'Hillieri'
   M. 'Hopa'
   M. hupehensis
   M. ioensis
   M. 'Profusion'
   M. spectabilis
Prunus conradinae
   P. mahaleb

P. pseudocerasus 'Cantabrigiensis'
P. speciosa
P. 'Wadai'
P. × *yedoensis*
Prunus, Japanese cherries,
   especially: 'Amanogawa'
   'Jo-nioi' 'Shirotae' 'Taki-nioi'
Robinia pseudoacacia
Styrax japonica
Tilia cordata
   T. × *euchlora*
   T. × *europaea*
   T. petiolaris
   T. platyphyllos

SHRUBS WITH FRAGRANT FLOWERS

Abelia chinensis
Azara microphylla
Berberis buxifolia
   B. sargentiana
Buddleia asiatica
   B. auriculata
   B. davidii & cvs
   B. fallowiana
   B. globosa
   B. 'Lochinch'
   B. madagascariensis
Camellia sasanqua & cvs
Cassinia fulvida

Chimonanthus praecox
Choisya ternata
Citrus spp
Clerodendrum bungei
   C. trichotomum
Clethra alnifolia
   C. delavayi
Cornus mas
Corokia cotoneaster
   C. virgata
Coronilla glauca
   C. valentina
Corylopsis spp

Cytisus battandieri
   C. × *praecox*
Daphne spp.
Deutzia 'Avalanche'
   D. compacta
   D. × *elegantissima*
Elaeagnus × *ebbingei*
   E. macrophylla
Erica arborea
   E. arborea 'Alpina'
Eupatorium weinmannianum
Freylinia lanceolata
Genista cinerea

G. fragrans
Hamamelis mollis & cvs
Hebe speciosa & hybds.
Ligustrum quihoui
Lonicera fragrantissima
   L. × *purpusii*
   L. standishii
   L. syringantha
Lupinus arboreus
Magnolia denudata
   M. sieboldii
   M. sinensis
   M. × *watsonii*
   M. wilsonii
Mahonia japonica
Myrtus communis
   M. luma

Osmanthus × *burkwoodii*
   O. decorus
   O. delavayi
   O. heterophyllus
Osmaronia cerasiformis
Philadelphus argyrocalyx
   P. coronarius & cvs
   P. delavayi
   P. microphyllus
   and named cvs
Pittosporum tenuifolium
Prunus mume & cvs
Rhododendron: many spp & hybrids
Ribes alpinum
   R. odoratum
Romneya spp
Rosa: many spp. & hybrids

Salix triandra
Sarcococca spp
Skimmia japonica 'Fragrans'
   S. japonica 'Rubella'
Spartium junceum
Syringa spp
   Syringa vulgaris cvs
Viburnum × *bodnantense* & cvs
   V. × *burkwoodii*
   V. × *carlcephalum*
   V. carlesii & cvs
   V. farreri & cvs
   V. foetens
   V. grandiflorum
   V. × *juddii*

TREES WITH AROMATIC BARK, WOOD OR LEAVES

Calycanthus spp
Cercidiphyllum (fallen leaves)
Chimonanthus praecox
Drimys winteri
Eucalyptus spp
Juglans spp

Laurus nobilis
Liquidambar styraciflua
Magnolia salicifolia
Populus × *acuminata*
   P. balsamifera
   P. × *candicans*

P. trichocarpa
Salix triandra
Umbellularia californica
   and most conifers

SHRUBS WITH AROMATIC FOLIAGE

Aloysia triphylla
Artemisia arborescens
Caryopteris spp & hybrids
Cistus × *aguilari*
   C × *cyprius*
   C. ladanifer
   C. palhinhae
   C. × *purpureus*
Drimys lanceolata
Elsholtzia stauntonii
Gaultheria procumbens
Hebe cupressoides

Helichrysum italicum
   H. plicatum
Hypericum 'Hidcote'
Lavandula spica
Myrtus communis
Olearia ilicifolia
   O. mollis
   O. moschata
Osmanthus ledifolius
Perovskia spp
Prostanthera spp
Rhododendron cinnabarinum

R. glaucophyllum
R. oreotrephes
R. saluenense
Rosmarinus officinalis
Ruta graveolens
Salvia grahamii
   S. neurepia
   S. rutilans
Santolina spp
Skimmia spp
Thymus spp

CLIMBERS WITH FRAGRANT FLOWERS

Clematis armandii
  C. cirrhosa balearica
  C. flammula
  C. montana
  C. rehderiana
Holboellia latifolia
Jasminum azoricum

J. officinale
J. polyanthum
J. × *stephanense*
Lonicera × *americana*
  L. caprifolium
  L. etrusca
  L. × *heckrotii*

L. japonica & cvs
L. periclymenum & cvs
Mandevilla suaveolens
Roses, many
Stauntonia hexaphylla
Trachelospermum spp
Wattakaka sinensis
Wisteria spp

HERBACEOUS PLANTS WITH FRAGRANT FLOWERS

Cestrum parqui
Chrysanthemum
Clematis heracleifolia & cvs
Convallaria majalis
Cosmos atrosanguineus
Dahlia
Delphinium wellbyi
Dianthus: pinks and carnations
Filipendula ulmaria
Helleborus lividus
Hemerocallis citrina
  H. dumortieri
  H. flava

H. middendorfiana
H. multiflora
  and yellow-flowered named cvs
Hosta 'Honeybells'
  H. plantaginea
  H. 'Royal Standard'
Iris florentina
  I. germanica
  I. graminea
  I. hoogiana
  I. pallida dalmatica
  I. unguicularis
Mirabilis jalapa

Paeonia (some)
Phlox: border cvs
  P. maculata & cvs
Primula alpicola
  P. florindae
  P. secundiflora
  P. sikkimensis
Romneya coulteri
  R. trichocalyx
Smilacina racemosa
Verbena bonariensis
  V. corymbosa
Yucca filamentosa

HERBACEOUS PLANTS WITH AROMATIC LEAVES

Acorus calamus
Anthemis nobilis
Artemisia spp
Calamintha grandiflora
  C. nepetoides
Dictamnus albus
Dracocephalum spp
Elsholtzia stauntonii

Foeniculum vulgare
Geranium macrorrhizum
Houttynia cordata
Leontopodium aloysiodorum
Melissa officinalis
Mentha spp, especially:
  M. pulegium
  M. requienii

Monarda didyma
Nepeta × *faassenii*
Perovskia spp
Salvia candidissima
  S. microphylla
  S. rutilans
Teucrium hyrcanicum
Thymus spp

Hyacinths can be enjoyed indoors for a season, then planted out to flower outside year after year.

ANNUALS AND BIENNIALS WITH FRAGRANT FLOWERS

Abronia spp
Alyssum maritimum
Centaurea moschata
Cheiranthus cheiri
Erysimum capitatum
Exacum affine

Humea elegans
Iberis spp
Ionopsidium acaule
Lathyrus odoratus
Limnanthes douglasii
Lupinus (annual kinds)

Matthiola
Oenothera biennis
Reseda odorata
Scabiosa atropurpurea
Schizopetalum walkeri
Tropaeolum (nasturtiums)

BULBS, CORMS ETC. WITH FRAGRANT FLOWERS

Amaryllis belladonna
Crinum spp
Crocus spp
Cyclamen persicum
Freesia refracta
Galanthus (many)
Galtonia candicans
Gladiolus callianthus

G. tristis
Hedychium spp
Hymenocallis spp
Iris reticulata
Lilium (many)
Muscari spp
Narcissus jonquilla
N. poeticus

N. triandrus
  and many named kinds
Polianthes tuberosa
Tulipa clusiana
T. sylvestris
  and some named kinds

BY WAY OF WARNING: PLANTS THAT DON'T SMELL GOOD

Clerodendrum spp: leaves smell of burnt rubber
Codonopsis: some spp smell of fox
Cotoneaster: flowers of many smell of boiled fish
Crataegus: flowers of many smell fishy
Dracunculus vulgaris: flowers smell of rotting meat
Escallonia illinita } plant smells
E. viscosa } of pigs

Fritillaria imperialis: crown imperials smell of fox
Ligustrum ovalifolium } privets
L. vulgare } smell sickly
              to many
Melianthus major: leaves smell of peanut butter
Phuopsis stylosa: plant smells of garlic and fox
Pyracantha (except *P. rogersiana*): flowers smell fishy

Salvia sclarea turkestanica: nicknamed 'hot housemaid'
Sambucus spp: flowers of elder smell sickly to some
Sorbus: flowers of rowans and whitebeams smell fishy
Stranvaesia: flowers smell fishy

PLANTS FOR CLAY SOILS

Abelia chinensis
Aesculus spp
Berberis spp
Choisya ternata
Cytisus × *praecox*
Deutzia spp
Eucalyptus spp
Fraxinus ornus
Genista spp

Hamamelis spp
Hypericum 'Hidcote'
Laburnum spp
Lonicera spp
Magnolia spp
Mahonia spp
Malus spp
Osmanthus spp
Philadelphus spp

Populus spp
Prunus spp
Pyracantha rogersiana
Ribes spp
Rosa spp & hybrids
Skimmia japonica
Tilia spp
Viburnum spp

PLANTS FOR CHALK SOILS

Aesculus spp
Alyssum maritimum
Buddleia davidii
  B. globosa
Cheiranthus cheiri
Dianthus
Erysimum spp
Fraxinus ornus
Hesperis matronalis
Iberis spp

Laurus nobilis
Lavandula spp
Ligustrum quihoui
Lilium regale
Lonicera spp
Magnolia grandiflora
M. × *highdownensis*
M. wilsonii
Malus spp
Nepeta spp

Oenothera spp
Olearia spp
Philadelphus spp & hybrids
Populus spp
Romneya spp
Rosa (many)
Salvia spp
Sarcococca spp
Spartium junceum
Syringa spp & cvs

PLANTS FOR DRY SOILS

Alyssum maritimum
Berberis buxifolia
  B. sargentiana
Buddleia spp
Cistus spp

Cytisus spp
Genista spp
Hebe cupressoides
Ligustrum quihoui
Lonicera spp

Lupinus arboreus
Rosa spinosissima
Rosmarinus officinalis
Spartium junceum

PLANTS NEEDING ACID SOIL

Camellia sasanqua
Clethra spp

Gaultheria procumbens
Magnolia spp (most)

Rhododendron

PLANTS FOR SHADE

Convallaria majalis
Daphne laureola
D. pontica
Elaeagnus spp

Gaultheria procumbens
Hemerocallis spp
Ionopsidium acaule
Limnanthes douglasii

Osmanthus spp
Rhododendron spp
Sarcococca spp
Smilacina racemosa

PLANTS FOR SEASIDE GARDENS

Acacia dealbata
Aloysia triphylla
Azara microphylla
Buddleia spp
Caryopteris spp
Choysia ternata
Clematis flammula
Coronilla valentina
Daphne mezereum
    D.odora
Dianthus
Elaeagnus spp
Genista spp

Iberis spp
Jasminum spp
Laurus nobilis
Lavandula spp
Lupinus arboreus
Myrtus spp
Nepeta spp
Oenothera spp
Olearia spp
Rosmarinus officinalis
Santolina spp
Spartium junceum
Skimmia japonica 'Fragrans'

S. japonica 'Rubella'
Smilacina racemosa
Syringa spp & cvs
Tilia spp
Thymus spp (many)
Viburnum × *bodnantense*
    V. × *burkwoodii*
    V. × *carlcephalum*
    V. carlesii
    V. farreri
    V. × *juddii*
Viola odorata
Wisteria spp

PLANTS FOR COLD GARDENS

Aesculus spp
Buddleia davidii
Calamintha grandiflora
Calycanthus spp
Centaurea moschata
Cheiranthus cheiri
Clematis flammula
    C. heracleifolia
    C. montana
Convallaria majalis
Corylopsis spicata
Daphne blagayana
    D. cneorum
    D. mezereum
    D. pontica
    D. retusa

Deutzia compacta
    D.sieboldiana
Dianthus barbatus
Filipendula ulmaria
Fraxinus ornus
Galanthus spp
Galtonia candicans
Gaultheria procumbens
Hamamelis spp
Hemerocallis flava
Hesperis matronalis
Iris graminea
    I. pallida
    I. reticulata
Jasminum officinale
Laburnum spp

Ligustrum quihoui
Lilium candidum
    L. regale
Lonicera spp (most)
Magnolia sinensis
    M. × *soulangiana*
Malus spp
Matthiola spp
Melissa officinalis
Monarda didyma
Muscari spp
Narcissus spp
Nepeta × *faassenii*
Oenothera biennis
Osmanthus × *burkwoodii*
Philadelphus spp & cvs

Phlox maculata
  P. paniculata cvs
Populus spp
Primula florindae

P. sikkimensis
P. veris
P. vulgaris
Ribes odoratum

Robinia pseudoacacia
Rosa spp & hybrids
Saponaria officinalis
Sarcococca spp

PLANTS FOR CONTAINERS & WINDOW BOXES

Alyssum maritimum
Anthemis nobilis
Cheiranthus spp
Crocus spp
Dianthus

Heliotropium peruvianum
Hyacinthus orientalis
Iris reticulata
Lilium spp
Matthiola spp

Muscari spp
Pelargonium spp & cvs with scented
  leaves
Reseda odorata

INDEX

Many of these plants will have different varieties described under their entry.

SOME NURSERIES IN THE U.K. WHERE FRAGRANT PLANTS MAY BE OBTAINED

Peter Beales Roses
London Road, Attleborough, Norfolk NR17 1AY
(old fashioned and some modern roses)

Bressingham Gardens
Diss, Norfolk IP22 2AB
(herbaceous plants)

Broadleigh Gardens
Barr House, Bishops Hull, Taunton, Somerset TA4 1AE
(bulbs)

Beth Chatto (Unusual Plants)
White Barn House, Elmstead Market, Colchester,
Essex CO7 7DB
(herbaceous plants)

Chiltern Seeds
Bortree Stile, Ulverston, Cumbria LA12 7PB
(seeds, inc. many tenders)

Cranborne Garden Centre
Cranborne, Wimborne, Dorset
(roses)

English Eucalyptus Blue Gums Garden Centre
The Quarter, Lamberhurst, Kent TN3 8AL
(eucalyptus)

Hillier Nurseries (Winchester) Ltd
Ampfield House, Ampfield, Nr Romsey,
Hampshire SO5 9PA
(shrubs and trees, also roses, herbaceous)

Iden Croft Herbs
Frittenden Road, Staplehurst, Kent TN12 0DH
(herbs)

De Jager
The Nurseries, Marden, Kent TN12 9BP
(bulbs inc. lilies, tenders)

Kingstone Cottage Plants
Weston under Penyard, Herefordshire HR9 7NX
(pinks and carnations, esp. old kinds)

W.G. & D.M. Maishman
Beauclere, Shellwood Cross, Reigate, Surrey RH2 8NZ
(sweet pea seed, inc. many old kinds)

Morehavens
Sway, Hampshire SO4 0EG
(chamomile 'Treneague')

Norfolk Lavender Ltd
Caley Hill, Heacham, King's Lynn, Norfolk PE31 7JE
(lavender)

Notcutts Nurseries Ltd
Woodbridge, Suffolk IP12 4AF
(shrubs and trees, lilacs, roses)

Peveril Nurseries,
Derril, Nr Holsworthy, Devon
(clematis)

Plants from the Past
The Old House, 1 North Street, Belhaven,
Dunbar EH42 1NU
(old-fashioned flowers, inc. dianthus)

Ramparts Nurseries
Bakers Lane, Colchester, Essex CO4 5BD
(silver and grey plants, inc. many aromatic; dianthus)

Roses du Temps Passé
Woodlands House, Stretton, Staffordshire ST19 9LG
(old roses)

Rougham Hall Nurseries
1 Ipswich Road, Rougham, Bury St Edmunds,
Suffolk IP30 9LZ
(herbaceous inc. phlox; seed of wallflower strains)

Elizabeth Smith
Downside, Bowling Green, Constantine, Falmouth,
Cornwall TR11 5AP
(violets)

Stillingfleet Lodge Nurseries
Stillingfleet, i.e. City of York
(fragrant and grey foliage plants)

Westfield Plants
Great Chalfield, Melksham, Wiltshire SN12 8NN
(mainly shrubs and trees, many unusual and tender kinds)